BEHOLD THE MAN!

*An Anthropological Comparison of the
Christologies of John Macquarrie
and of Wolfhart Pannenberg*

Marion Lars Hendrickson

University Press of America,® Inc.
Lanham • New York • Oxford

BT
198
. H445
1998

Copyright © 1998 by
University Press of America,® Inc.
4720 Boston Way
Lanham, Maryland 20706

12 Hid's Copse Rd.
Cummor Hill, Oxford OX2 9JJ

Library of Congress Cataloging-in-Publication Data

Hendrickson, Marion Lars.
Behold the man! : an anthropological comparison of the christologies
of John Macquarrie and of Wolfhart Pannenberg / Marion Lars
Hendrickson.
Originally presented as the author's thesis (master of sacred
theology)—Nashotah House.
p.   cm.
Includes bibliographical references and index.
1. Jesus Christ—History of doctrines—20th century. 2. Man
(Christian theology)—History of doctrines—20th century. 3.
Theology—Methodology—History of doctrines—20th century 4.
Macquarrie, John. 5. Pannenberg, Wolfhart, 1928-. I. Title.
BT198.H445 1998   232'.092'2—dc21   98-2651 CIP

ISBN 0-7618-1049-8 (cloth: alk. ppr.)

To the memory of my first teachers,
Lars and Norma Hendrickson

For tronen stå
Med kroner på
I himlens prestedrakt!

Contents

Preface

This is a little book with large aspirations. To grapple with the inter-relationship of Jesus Christ, humanity and the theological insights of John Macquarrie and of Wolfhart Pannenberg has been daunting and delightful at the same time. This study is akin to the aeolian harp, whose tempered strings are enlivened by the various breezes passing through them, now softly, now more briskly. As a pastor and theologian formed in the confessional Lutheran orthodoxy of The Lutheran Church—Missouri Synod I have discovered the Christological *loci* of this tradition enlivened in sympathetic and surprising ways by Macquarrie's and Pannenberg's writings. I leave it to the reader to judge the effects of this music.

Since the book is a published form of my thesis, the culmination of my studies for the Master of Sacred Theology degree at Nashotah House in Nashotah, Wisconsin, there are several people who have contributed to this work. I am deeply grateful to the community of The Mission for making this Wittenberger feel welcomed in Canterbury. Particular acknowledgment and gratitude are due to Nashotah professors Fr. Ralph McMichael, my thesis director, and Fr. Charles Miller, reader, whose comments and guidance provided discipline and encouragement. My deep thanks are given to Professor John Macquarrie whose instruction as a guest lecturer at Nashotah was profoundly thought-provoking, and whose personal encouragement helped refine this present work and also lead to its publication. For this latter event I am grateful to the University Press of America, Inc.

A special word of thanks is due to the congregation of St. Peter's Lutheran Church, Arlington, Wisconsin, for the kind allowance to pursue my studies while providing them with pastoral care. And finally to my wife, Connie, and sons, Matthew and Michael, who shared their husband and father with this project, I am indebted to their loving encouragement and patience.

Marion L. Hendrickson
The Nativity of our Lord, 1997

vii

Acknowledgments

The author gratefully acknowledges the use of the following copyrighted material:

In Search of Humanity: A Theological and Philosophical Approach by John Macquarrie. Copyright © 1982 by John Macquarrie. Used with permission of The Crossroad Publishing Company, New York, and SCM Press, Ltd., London

Jesus Christ in Modern Thought by John Macquarrie. Copyright © 1990 by SCM Press, Ltd. Used by permission of SCM Press, Ltd. and Trinity Press International.

Jesus—God and Man by Wolfhart Pannenberg. Copyright © 1968, 1977 by The Westminster Press. Used by permission of Westminster John Knox Press and SCM Press, Ltd.

Systematic Theology, Volume 2 by Wolfhart Pannenberg. Copyright © 1994 by Wm. B. Eerdmans Publishing Co. Used by permission of Wm. B. Eerdmans Publishing Co.

Chapter 1

Introduction

I. Anthropology as the Starting Point

"*Was ist das?*" "What does this mean?" This is the recurring question in Martin Luther's *Small Catechism* which frames his theological explanations of basic Christian doctrine. For the Reformer, what is seen is not always the obvious answer. God, as *deus absconditus*, cloaks himself in contradiction. Thus questions about the glory of God are answered in the flesh of humanity, in suffering, in death—the cross. Questions and their answers still challenge the contemporary theologians John Macquarrie and Wolfhart Pannenberg.

For John Macquarrie the question is not *Was* but *Wer*, not *What* but *Who*. "Who are you?" He asks this question of humanity, of God and of Jesus Christ. But to whom the question is first put and how that first answer impacts the response of the others is the task Macquarrie takes up. "If we can begin from the humanity which we all share, and if we find that this humanity points beyond itself for its completion, then we have, so to speak, indicated the place of the word 'God' on the map of meaningful discourse."[1]

Wolfhart Pannenberg also believes a discussion of humanity is the starting point for theology. "...in the modern age anthropology has become not only in fact but also with objective necessity the terrain on which theologians must base their claim of universal validity for what they say."[2]

This having been said, that the *who* concerning God begins with answering the *who* concerning humanity, can the Christian theologian answer the question *who* concerning humanity without referring to the *who* of God? Here is the place for Christology. Christian theology and anthropology can be bound together in Christology. This binding together of anthropology, theology and Christology creates tensions. These tensions are compounded when two theologians and their treatments of this three-fold reality are compared. It is "the inescapable element of paradox that enters into all theological language... Even in discussing the nature of man, we [are] very much aware of the tensions and oppositions. But the element of paradox reaches its highest pitch...in the doctrine of the God-man."[3]

Like Luther's classic statement of the Christian existence—*simul justus et peccator*—there will be opposites in tension throughout the considerations in this book. The theological task, however, is just such a challenge: to treat each issue fully and simultaneously. Such discussions, "contradictory when taken for themselves, are meaningful only when they are *not* taken for themselves but are understood in their connection with their basis in the event of God's revelation in Jesus."[4]

Similarly, then, the purpose of this book is not to develop a synthesis of Macquarrie's and Pannenberg's thought; rather it is to place each theologian side by side to gain a fuller understanding of Christology and anthropology. The anthropological field upon which this work will compare the two theologians' thought is essential, as stated earlier, to explicate a fully human Jesus to human beings, and what this fully human Jesus reveals about God. Such a comparison is encouraged by Macquarrie's and Pannenberg's mutual starting points—anthropology—contrasted by their diverging methods—existentialism in Macquarrie, metaphysics in Pannenberg. The two sections which follow below briefly present the childhood years, education and teaching experiences of Macquarrie and of Pannenberg.[5] The fourth section will outline the chapters to follow.

II. A Biographical Sketch of John Macquarrie

"Probably most theologians experience a tension in their work. I have known one from the beginning."[6] The "beginning" to which John Macquarrie refers is the beginning of his theological training in 1936 at Glasgow University in Scotland. Yet the tension existed from childhood.

Born June 27, 1919, in Renfew, Scotland, John Macquarrie was heir to a hard-working Scottish family line. His father, John, was a skilled shipyard worker in the city of Glasgow. Macquarrie's grandfather, from the Isle of Islay, also worked near Scotland's industrial giant.

In the parental home of John and Robina Macquarrie, young John was brought up in the Presbyterian Church of Scotland, nurtured with a sense of deep religious commitment. This commitment, guided by the elder John Macquarrie's leadership in the church, was balanced in tension with an openness and tolerance toward the convictions of others. "[Macquarrie] recognized early both the importance of religious convictions and the legitimacy of religious diversity."[7]

Formal education began in the Paisley Grammar School, followed by seven rigorous years at the University of Glasgow—four years toward the MA with honors, 1940, in mental philosophy, and three years for the BD, 1943. One of Macquarrie's professors at the University of Glasgow was Charles A. Campbell, Professor of Logic and Rhetoric. The logician had a profound influence on his student, demonstrating to him a common agreement in the nature of *suprarational* theism, the nature of religious language, together with the roles of philosophy and theology as they relate to the central role of experience in religion.[8]

Macquarrie himself, reflecting on his early education, points to his study of the writings of F. H. Bradley, as the one philosopher "who really bowled me over."[9] "I found his idea of the suprarational Absolute very congenial... I followed him too in his thinking that the doctrines of Christianity...are symbols of eternal truth."[10]

The three years of studying theology were not as stimulating for Macquarrie as his four years of rigorous philosophical training. "Calvin and Barth I found insufferable."[11] Completing the BD Degree in 1943, Macquarrie served as a chaplain in the British Army until 1948. Upon discharge he became the minister of St. Ninian's Church (Church of Scotland) in the northwest of Scotland, where he served faithfully, if not wholeheartedly.[12]

It was in 1953 that an "accidental" visit by a former theological professor vacationing near Macquarrie's parish led to Macquarrie's return to formal study. He became a lecturer in systematic theology at his alma mater, the University of Glasgow, while studying for the PhD Degree. There Macquarrie came under the influence of Ian Henderson who, as Macquarrie's thesis director, guided him into the subject of Heidegger's philosophical influence on Bultmann's theology. "[Henderson's] mind was both profound and acutely critical, and my theological pilgrimage owes more than I can express to his guidance and stimulation."[13]

Under Henderson's guidance Macquarrie's PhD thesis became his first book, *An Existentialist Theology* (1955). This work addressed the tension of Macquarrie's theological work along positive lines. The

Heidegger/Bultmann subject matter was more fruitful to Macquarrie than Bradley's philosophy of Macquarrie's undergraduate years. This new subject served to reconcile in Macquarrie's mind the tension of religious faith and intellectual integrity.

Following nine years of lecturing at Glasgow and writing on existential themes, Macquarrie crossed the Atlantic to a full professorship in Systematic Theology at Union Theological Seminary in New York. Here his creative tension in theology encompassed wider horizons. The writings of two Roman Catholic theologians caught the attention of a Macquarrie not quite satisfied with Bultmann's thought. Karl Rahner and Hans Urs von Balthasar helped Macquarrie "break out of a narrow existentialism."[14]

While at Union another long-standing tension in Macquarrie's theological life found new direction. On the one hand there was the "dreary evangelical Protestantism in which I had been raised."[15] On the other hand there was the "whole complex of theology and spirituality and a distinctive way of understanding the church"[16] which presented itself to Macquarrie in the tradition of the catholic writers, Rahner and von Balthasar. The result was Macquarrie's consummation of a "flirting affair" with the Anglican communion. He was ordained a deacon and then a priest of the Episcopal Church in 1965. "In becoming an Anglican I did not feel that I was erasing my past. Rather, I was taking it with me into something broader, richer, more fulfilling, more catholic."[17]

In 1966 Father Macquarrie set down his synthesis of catholic faith and reasonable philosophy in a single volume of systematic theology called *Principles of Christian Theology*. Eleven years later, following a decade of wrestling with the *New Theology* of the *Death of God* theologians, of advocating for a need for traditional Christian belief, and with a return to England where he had been appointed Lady Margaret Professor of Divinity at Oxford, Macquarrie revised and enlarged his systematics. As Lady Margaret Professor, Macquarrie officiated the daily office and celebrated the Eucharist at Christ Church, Oxford. This immersion in the liturgical life of the Church, coupled with his challenging the *New Theology*, moved Macquarrie to include more material in Christology for his revised *Principles*.

This new focus on Christology was not simply an intellectual focus. It grew out of Macquarrie's experiences as priest, professor and human being. "It has been my contention for a long time that the doctrine of man is the right starting point for contemporary theology...and necessary prolegomen[on] to the study of Christology."[18]

This contention led Macquarrie to write *In Search of Humanity* in 1982, unifying many different aspects of the human phenomenon. In 1984 a companion volume, *In Search of Deity*, clarified Macquarrie's conception of God in relation to his conception of human being. Having written these two books, Macquarrie felt the need to complete his humanity/deity prolegomena by the writing of a third study, on Christology. *Jesus Christ in Modern Thought* was published in 1990.

With this recent book and retirement, it would be inaccurate to conclude that the pilgrimage of John Macquarrie had reached its conclusion. "The life of the theologian will always be a pilgrimage with no stopping place that he or she can consider final. In what time remains to me, I shall carry on my quest for a Christian theology truly catholic and truly critical."[19] Macquarrie gives living testimony to his own words that a fruitful life in successful pursuit of the resolution of the creative tensions in theology "is not to decide in advance that it cannot go any further."[20]

III. A Biographical Sketch of Wolfhart Pannenberg

Wolfhart Pannenberg, nine years junior to John Macquarrie, travels a road similar to the Scot—a nurturing home, experience with the Second World War and a teaching career in which to work out an understanding of philosophy and theology through intellectual engagement. Yet the differences are as significant as the similarities.

Stettin, the city of Pannenberg's birth in 1928, was a German city in the province of Pomerania. Now it is part of Poland and Pannenberg mourns, "It is never without sadness that I remember the place of my birth, which seems so far away now."[21] The geo-political changes following World War II resulting in a distant homeland, became a sign of the mature thought of Pannenberg concerning past, present and future.

The Pannenberg home did not profess a devotional type of Christianity. The family left the church altogether in the 1930's.[22] At the age of seven Pannenberg began to study the piano. Music became so much an important part of the young Pannenberg's life that his father—a customs officer—feared that his son would neglect his school work. Still the young man went as often as he could to hear von Karajan and the Aachen symphony.

Schooling and music were soon overtaken by the war. Having moved from Stettin to Aachen in 1936, the Pannenberg family left Aachen in 1942 because of destruction from British bombing raids. It was on to Berlin where school was held in the safety of the country. By 1944 the family left its Berlin home because of the war's destruction, and returned to Pomerania to stay with relatives. It was during this time in Pomerania that Pannenberg chanced upon his first philosophy book. It was a little book of Nietzsche on music,[23] but it whetted an appetite in the musically-inclined Pannenberg to read everything he could find by that philosopher.

On January 6, 1945, the sixteen year old Pannenberg went through something of a mystical experience.

> While I was walking back home from school an extraordinary event occurred in which I found myself absorbed in the light of the setting sun and for one eternal moment dissolved in the light surrounding me. When I became aware again of my finite existence, I did not know what had happened but I certainly knew that it was the most important event of my life.[24]

In the waning months of the war, as the need for soldiers became critical, Pannenberg was pressed into service in the *Wehrmacht*. Illness kept him from the heaviest action where many colleagues were killed. The spring of 1945 saw Pannenberg captured by the British, held for the remaining weeks of the war, and released that summer. Understandably the experiences of the war intruding into the formative years of the young Pannenberg left a vivid experience in the young man concerning humanity.

With the upheavals of war now past, Pannenberg met the intellectual challenge of higher education. In 1947 he enrolled at the Humboldt University in Berlin where philosophy and theology were his focus. He was resolved to give meaning to the Epiphany of 1945. While at Humboldt he seriously studied Marxism, only later making a distinction between the intellectual brilliance of Marxism and its ideological oppression as a system of government.

In the fall of 1948 Pannenberg traveled to Göttingen for a year of study where his philosophical rigor was honed under the tutelage of Nicolai Hermann. On a World Council of Churches scholarship

Pannenberg was off to Basel, Switzerland, for a term. There his studies of Barth were guided and supplemented by Professor Karl Jaspers.

It was at Heidelberg in 1950 during Pannenberg's fourth year of theological study that major resolutions of his own developing thought were achieved. The impact of Gerhard von Rad was formative for Pannenberg's understanding of history as an indispensable element of human life. Furthermore, von Rad's insistence from Old Testament studies that Yahweh is bound to time would lead Pannenberg to understand all history as the self-revelation of God.

Hans von Campenhausen was another Heidelberg professor who had profound impact on Pannenberg. It was Campenhausen "who kindled my enthusiasm and admiration for Christian patristic theology."[25] This was an important influence for Pannenberg as he realized that the patristic writers did not segregate faith and reason. Campenhausen also reinforced the historical consciousness that von Rad created in Pannenberg's mind. Karl Löwith rounded out a triumvirate of influence at Heidelberg. His philosophy of history lectures linked modern history to biblical theology of history.

Pannenberg's own writing at this time was encouraged by his advisor, Edmund Schlink. Schlink introduced the mind of Pannenberg to elements of confessional Lutheranism, which Pannenberg considered too confining though still important. It was Schlink who also led Pannenberg to consider elements of other disciplines of study in relation to theology, notably the natural sciences. Schlink, too, encouraged Pannenberg to continue with further study in the area of systematic theology. Thus with the intellectual refinement at Heidelberg, Pannenberg now concluded that theology needed to be developed on as sophisticated a plane as the best of philosophy. This was a conclusion upon which he now acted through his teaching and writing career.

In 1958 Pannenberg began teaching systematic theology at the seminary of Wuppertal, leaving there in 1961 for the University of Mainz. During these teaching years anthropology and Christology were Pannenberg's focus. "I soon became persuaded that one first has to acquire a systematic account of every other field, not only theology, but also philosophy and the dialogue with the natural and social sciences before with sufficient confidence one can dare to develop the doctrine of God."[26] Pannenberg's first written works, *What Is Man?* (German version, 1962) and *Jesus—God and Man* (German version, 1964) reflected his anthropology/Christology prolegomena approach to the doctrine of God. A second edition of *Jesus—God and Man* in 1976 and Pannenberg's *Anthropology in Theological Perspective*, 1983, further developed his insights concerning Christology and anthropology.

A series of visiting professorships in the United States—Harvard, 1966, and Clarmont, 1967 and 1975—constituted a coalescing of philosophical ideas in Pannenberg's mind. These opportunities also aided Pannenberg's understanding of ecumenical issues and the interaction of many disciplines.

Still through all this time of lecturing and writing Pannenberg had maintained a provisional understanding of his own theological presentations. The definitive thought of Pannenberg's method was finally put into print with his three volume *Systematische Theologie*—the first volume appearing in 1988, all three of which consequently have appeared in English translation. With the writing of this mature exposition and with his retirement in 1995 Pannenberg has capped a systematic exposition of Christian theology with an understanding of his own personal history within the bigger sphere of human/divine history. It is at the end that reason and hope can grasp what has happened along the way. "True respect for the mystery [the mystery of God and the mystery of Pannenberg's own human life experiences, both revealed in time] can express itself, among other ways, just in the attempt to understand it fully."[27] *To understand* has been the driving force of the life and thought of Wolfhart Pannenberg.

IV. The Outline of Chapters to Follow

The second chapter of this book will be devoted to Macquarrie's thought on anthropology, theology and Christology. For the chapter to allow Macquarrie to speak fully, his own line of argument will form the outline of the chapter. Beginning with a study of the different aspects of human life (Macquarrie's anthropology), it will be shown that the study of humanity directs one to the spiritual reality which is the source, support and goal of humanity (Macquarrie's theology). The resulting point of contact between the anthropological and theological studies will be the man Jesus (Macquarrie's Christology). Following this outline of anthropology-theology-Christology, Macquarrie's thought will be most effectively outlined in preparation for comparison with Pannenberg's.

For the third chapter, devoted to Pannenberg's Christology—which one may call anthropological theology or empirical metaphysics—discussion will begin with an outline of Pannenberg's method for systematic theology. His strong emphasis on method must first be addressed to lay the foundation for his thought concerning the issues in this book. Having set this methodological base the chapter will turn to Christology as the center for anthropology and theology.

The chapter then will provide a parallel discussion of how the issues of Christology impact both humanity and divinity at the same time. The purpose of such a parallel discussion is to present the tension in Pannenberg's thought. For while method and anthropology are starting points for him, Christology, anthropology and theology are held in tension throughout Pannenberg's thought.

The fourth chapter of this work will compare the similarities and differences between Macquarrie and Pannenberg, as well as offer critical reflection. The similarities between the two theologians which will be discussed in this concluding chapter include: 1) a Christology *from below*, 2) a continuity with the Christological confessions of the early Church, especially Chalcedon, 3) a desire to make the issues of anthropology, theology and Christology intelligible to the present human mind, and 4) an insistence that the Christ of faith and the Jesus of history be kept united.

The issues on which Macquarrie and Pannenberg differ will then be discussed. The first issue relates to the respective systems of the two theologians. John Macquarrie's ontological-existentialism advocates a world of thought with an open future. His discussions of transcendence result in an always moving beyond one's self for both humanity and divinity. Wolfhart Pannenberg, on the other hand, with his proleptic eschatology has a fixed goal toward which humanity and divinity move, while avoiding any rigid fatalism.

The second issue upon which the two theologians differ relates to the first issue. In Macquarrie's Christology it is the death of Jesus that is significant—significant for both humanity and divinity, echoing Heidegger's philosophy. To address transcendence and a future that is open, death is the primary issue to be considered. For Pannenberg, with his eschatological focus, it is the resurrection of Jesus from the dead that is the significant event. The resurrection is the future unfolding in present time. It is, for Pannenberg, *the* issue that shapes both human future and God's future.

The final issue will be the conclusions each theologian draws about humanity as reflected from Christology. Do their differing methods in fact begin from the same place, or do their differences reveal that the starting point is not something they hold in common? And, as the title of this book implies, what sort of people—human and Christian—are we today?

Notes

1. John Macquarrie, *Studies in Christian Existentialism* (London: SCM Press, Ltd., 1965), 327.

2. Wolfhart Pannenberg, *Anthropology in Theological Perspective* (Philadelphia: Westminster Press, 1968), 16.

3. John Macquarrie, *Principles of Christian Theology*, 2nd ed. (New York: Charles Scribner's Sons, 1977), 306.

4. Wolfhart Pannenberg, *Jesus—God and Man* (Philadelphia: Westminster Press, 1968), 183.

5. While this anthropological comparison of the Christologies of Macquarrie and Pannenberg will consider the ideas appropriate to each man's work, still ideas are not autonomous. The ideas developed by each theologian are part of their personal histories. Their theological output is refracted through the particular blend of experiences and thoughts that make each man.

6. Alister Kee & Eugene T. Long, editors, *Being and Truth: Essays in Honor of John Macquarrie* (London: SCM Press, Ltd., 1986), xi.

7. Eugene T. Long, *Existence, Being and God* (New York: Paragon House Publishers, 1985), 1.

8. Ibid., 3; cf. Charles A. Campbell, *On Selfhood and Godhead*.

9. Kee & Long, *Being and Truth*, xii.

10. Ibid.

11. Ibid.

12. Kee & Long, *Being and Truth*, xii.

13. Ibid., xiii.

14. Ibid., xiv.

15. Ibid., x.

16. Ibid., xii.

17. Ibid., xv

18. Ibid., xvii-xviii.

19. Ibid., xviii.

20. John Macquarrie, *Jesus Christ in Modern Thought* (London: SCM Press, Ltd., 1990), 343.

21. Carl E. Braaten & Philip Clayton, editors, *The Theology of Wolfhart Pannenberg* (Minneapolis: Augsburg Publishing House, 1988), 11.

22. Ibid., 13.

23. *The Birth of Tragedy from the Spirit of Music*, Nietzsche's first book, 1872, mentioned by Pannenberg in Braaten & Clayton, *The Theology of Wolfhart Pannenberg*, 12.

24. Braaten & Clayton, *The Theology of Wolfhart Pannenberg*, 12.

25. Ibid., 15.

26. Ibid., 16.

27. Stanley Grenz, *Reason for Hope: The Systematic Theology of Wolfhart Pannenberg* (New York: Oxford University Press, 1990), 43.

Chapter 2

John Macquarrie

I. Introduction — To Become To Be Human

"The being of man, this very entity which exists in the light of Being...becomes the symbol for Being itself."[1] John Macquarrie's sentence is brief, but it speaks volumes. He writes of human "being," "existing" and "becoming." "Being" implies a static state for man. "Becoming" implies a process of change. Thus "the first obvious complexity in this study of the human, and a major source of elusiveness is that we have to concern ourselves with the possibilities as well as the actuality."[2] In Macquarrie's mind the former is simpler for study than the latter. Therefore in his book, *In Search of Humanity*, Macquarrie opens with a discussion of "becoming" human and closes with a chapter on human "being." In the paradox of becoming what one already is, the intervening chapters form an extended discussion of the elements of human becoming/being.

The choice of emphasizing Macquarrie's book, *In Search of Humanity*, is an important one. This book grew out of a series of lectures given by Macquarrie in the late 1970s. In attempting to present the various aspects or attributes of human beings and relate these attributes to each other, Macquarrie gave expression to his convictions about anthropology, theology and Christology. "It has been my contention for a long time that the doctrine of man is the right starting point for a contemporary theology."[3] As mentioned in the previous chapter, this book, *In Search of Humanity*, is the first of a trilogy of books clarifying Macquarrie's periodical writings and earlier works.[4]

While the book is a unified study of human attributes arranged between "Becoming" and "Being," Macquarrie emphasizes various groupings of the attributes in their interrelations. These sub-groupings will be identified by the titles of the sub-sections of this chapter— fundamental attributes which are explicated by other attributes; interactive attributes which involve the human being in relation to others; alienation, the attribute which has a significance that necessitates a solo emphasis; the ethical and play, a set of attributes that interact especially with each other; and finally the austere attributes, called such not in a negative sense but in the sense of the profound role they play in human existence. While these sub-groupings are not overtly identified by Macquarrie in the chapter outlines of his unified book, the groupings are implied very clearly in Macquarrie's discussions of the attributes of humanity.

The opening chapter alone, however, is more than mere anthropology. There is something which Macquarrie, following Heidegger, dubs "Being." Yet in his study of humanity, it is only at the end that human becoming will be seen to be "stamped with Being."[5] "Surely there is some link between the humanity of God and the humanity we know on earth. If so, then our ordinary everyday humanity must afford on the finite level some clue, however distant, of the being of God."[6] In his own way, Macquarrie is giving thought to the words of Genesis: "Then God said, 'Let us make man in our image, after our likeness.'" (Genesis 1:26) For Macquarrie the Genesis verse is the conclusion based on an examination of humanity; an examination that yields implications for the presence of a divine image in humanity.[7] First, however, comes a discussion of human becoming/being. In this discussion it will be seen how "the light of Being" becomes *ensymboled* in humanity.

II. The Attributes of Humanity

The Fundamental Attributes

There are a number of attributes in humanity that reflect human "becoming" at the same time that they are the means to "becoming" more human. "The fundamental human freedom is to create humanity itself."[8] For humanity to become more fully human necessitates a freedom to do so. It is a freedom to think, to decide, to act, to experience, to become. Yet freedom is not a thing in humanity that has its own idiomatic properties capable of analysis and description. Rather, freedom is "the absence of constraints, it is an open space not yet filled up."[9] In understanding freedom in this way Macquarrie sees a creative force in the hands of humanity. To create *ex nihilo* something new is at the heart of freedom.[10] For freedom to be freedom it begins with nothing—no pre-determined parameters, no limits, no foregone conclusions.

Closely related to the primordial attribute of freedom is the attribute of transcendence. Transcendence is more often considered a divine attribute, but Macquarrie attributes it to humanity. It issues from the attribute of freedom in an on-going process of creativity. In this process humanity becomes more human. This "more" is to be understood in a qualitative sense, not quantitatively.

Human beings are capable of transcending time by considering the past and the future in present thought. Interaction with the natural world and history also involves transcendence, as does interpersonal relationships within the social order. In each and in many other domains transcendence is "a deepening, enhancing or enriching of life...a fuller, truer humanizing of life."[11]

Now freedom, the primordial ground out of which transcendence springs, is guided by something. It is guided, not by determinism, but rather by the free human ego, the *I*. "Egoity," the state of being an ego or self, is not a substantial state in the ancient understanding of a substantial soul.[12] Macquarrie prefers the term "leading edge," from the Greek *hegemonikon*, as a better understanding of ego.[13] "Leading edge" captures the attributes of freedom and transcendence in that ego is defined as "the conscious, rational, discriminating, unifying, purposeful element in the human being that leads us in one direction rather than another."[14] It is the thinking/acting combination, a reflecting/choosing, which keeps ego from becoming egoism. Egoism is the consciousness of self that turns in upon the self, whereas egoity is the consciousness of self which works in concert with transcendence and freedom.

Macquarrie completes his first unit of human fundamental attributes by embodying freedom, transcendence and egoity in flesh. He qualifies the notion of embodied humanity in two ways. First, it is not a denial of freedom and transcendence. The body is not inherently a limit, a predeterminism or bondage for the ego/self, any more than egoity is a limit to freedom and transcendence. Rather, just as egoity is the "leading edge" or directing thought of the human being, so the body is a necessary attribute, in combination with the other attributes, toward positive human becoming. Secondly, it is important to note that the human body is not merely an appendage or shell for the self. Macquarrie will permit no dualism here between body and soul.[15]

The embodiedment of freedom, transcendence and egoity is integral to the perpetuating of these same attributes. The body provides sensation, emotion, desire and relations to others that are vital for the thought/choosing of egoity, for the "moving beyond to something more" of transcendence and for the creative work of freedom. Furthermore, the embodiedment of humanity is itself an attribute of becoming. For while human beings are embodied selves, there remains a becoming more so. The "psychosomatic" unity of human beings, as Macquarrie prefers to call it, still has the task of synthesizing the different conflicting tendencies within the human person leading to a transcending of the present into something more.

This first unit of attributes receives further division and elaboration into other attributes of humanity. Before going further, however, it would be in order to consider objections to what Macquarrie has said. Macquarrie himself provides such a discussion by raising hypothetical objections to what he has stated. In regard to the fundamental attributes, Macquarrie raises objections concerning limits. Is human freedom not indeed limited, and if it is limited is it truly free? Does not the limiting of freedom, then, also limit transcendence and the self and the body?

Macquarrie does not evade his hypothetical charge. He embraces it. "Freedom is always hemmed in and limited."[16] Human beings in each generation do not start from scratch. Freedom may indeed be called an attribute *ex nihilo*, but this *out of nothing* is not absolute. A human being's freedom is limited by temperament, aptitude and intelligence. One's place in history, in the social order and in economic standing also limits choices and therefore limits freedom. Past choices, both good and foolish, create limits within which any future choices may be made. "The stubborn element of the given remains alongside freedom, to condition, limit and even frustrate it."[17]

For Macquarrie the solution is found in transcendence. As freedom is clearly not an absolute attribute, neither is it an attribute in a vacuum. Rather freedom, meeting the limits to this attribute, is carried further by transcending those limits in a new way. (Or negatively, the limit turns freedom back into a humanity-denying oppression.)[18] Thus it is the paradoxical tension of freedom and limit that impels transcendence.

The same line of argument can answer the limits to transcendence. For if every horizon cannot be surpassed does this not deny transcendence? Once again Macquarrie sees the solution in the paradox.

If transcending humanity confronts an unsurpassable horizon, the thought or desire to surpass it has already in fact transcended that horizon, even if the deed of transcending has yet to follow. Since the thought/desire/dream of the ego is the "leading edge," then deeds are likely to follow in time.

Nevertheless, granting that in each of the attributes mentioned thus far the limits do in fact combine with the attribute in a paradox of potential, does not the embodiedment of humanity create the *ne plus ultra*?[19] The flesh is highly limited by time, space and circumstances. Ultimately the flesh is limited by death. Yet the limits of finitude and death are paradoxically combined with human becoming, creating in the light of profound limitation—death—all the potential for a more truly human living. "Death...becomes creative of self-hood."[20]

It might be argued that the fundamental attributes discussed above are simply modifications of animal life. Macquarrie recognizes that "human beings are descended from animal ancestors and still resemble animals in many ways."[21] Yet there is something in the human being that, while seemingly indistinguishable from the same phenomenon of animals, is a phenomenon of a different order. The next set of attributes will bring this to light.

The Interactive Attributes[22]

In Macquarrie's study, *In Search of Humanity*, he follows his consideration of the fundamental attributes with four attributes of a more subtle nature. These he labels "Cognition," "Having," "Sociality" and "Language." Each of these attributes builds on those attributes already discussed. The attributes in this section are called interactive (a term implied in Macquarrie's writing) because the human being, to be truly human, is a subject in the world, not isolated from it. "If we isolate [the activities of human beings], we turn the human being in all his concreteness into the abstraction of a knowing subject not so much in the world as over against it...That is something less than a human being."[23]

The first of these attributes is cognition. "Cognition is essential to human transcendence."[24] As discussed earlier in conjunction with the attribute of egoity there is a whole range of critical thinking and reflection that goes on in human becoming. This cognition yields knowledge that is much more than the narrow sense-oriented knowledge called empiricism. While Macquarrie will tolerate no slighting of the significant role of empirical knowledge, he also sees no benefit from forcing all knowledge into an empirical frame of reference.[25]

Explicating the attribute of cognition, Macquarrie makes seven statements that challenge a narrow empiricism:

> 1. That some knowledge does *not* begin from observation.
> 2. That conjecture and imaginative hypotheses (even, and perhaps especially, improbable ones!) may be more fruitful than inductive generalizations.
> 3. That in many subjects, and not least in the study of humanity itself, the ideal of detachment is a hindrance.
> 4. That knowledge is a function of an active self participating in a world rather than data collected by an abstract thinking subject.
> 5. That there are various kinds of tacit knowledge, ranging all the way from the skills of craftsmanship to the insights of artists and even the visions of mystics, and these cannot be put into propositions expressed in clear and distinct ideas.
> 6. That knowledge of facts expressed in propositions is one kind of knowledge among others, and has to be considered in the context of more distinct forms of knowledge by participation, including knowledge of things, knowledge of other people and knowledge of ourselves.
> 7. That finally the concept of knowledge is far broader and richer than the narrower type of empiricist epistemology is prepared to concede.[26]

These seven statements, "which constitute a kind of manifesto for a more human concept of knowledge,"[27] will be put to use later in discussing Macquarrie's theology and answering criticisms of his methodology. However, in conjunction with anthropology, Macquarrie understands the attribute of cognition to be a valuable aid to transcendence, embracing all types of knowledge to create possibilities upon which to act in freedom. Knowledge in this light becomes more human—not more subjective—because it rests on a broader conception of reality.[28]

The attribute of having builds upon the attribute of embodiedment. Having reflects more than a simple relation to the material world. There is a participation in the things had. Yet like the dangers mentioned in connection with freedom—a limit to freedom serving either to advance transcendence or dehumanize the one who does not transcend the limit—having possessions can serve the becoming of the embodied self or dehumanize it. The latter is reflected in the saying, "The more things we possess, the more we are possessed by our things." Both a deprivation of things and a preoccupation with having things can dehumanize.

The attribute of having in regard to the material world mirrors the attribute of sociality in the interpersonal world. Here there exists a tension, not between the haves and the have nots, but between the individual and the community.[29] Macquarrie suggests four basic characters of human life which point to the social character of human beings. First, there is human sexuality. While animals are also male and female,

> the human sexual relation is never merely biological. It is a personal relation, and even when its personal dimension is minimized or almost obliterated, it does not revert to a biological relation but deteriorates to a subpersonal relation.[30]

The second character builds upon the first. Every human being belongs in a family. Compared with animals, human beings have a much longer period of dependence. While a child will grow in the freedom of independence, it is within the social context of the family that the growing freedom is enhanced by the members of that family.

Language is a third character. "The capacity for language... constitutes the main difference between man and the animals."[31] By its very nature language is a character shared with others. "No individual could have a language of his own."[32]

Finally, the human attribute of sociality is indicated by the character of economical interdependence. More than a repetition of the attribute of having, this character is seen by Macquarrie to be demonstrated by the division of labor among human beings. "We can only survive and enjoy a reasonable level of having through an intricate network of production, and this also stresses our solidarity and interdependence."[33]

Once again, like the dangers of having material possessions—dehumanization either through greed or through deprivation—sociality has dangers. "It is not good for the man to be alone." On the other hand, as soon as man creates social orders they take over with a life of their own, tyrannizing and dehumanizing human life.[34] The healthy balance is found in the tension of a clear *I* relating to a clear *Thou*. It is the life of the individual in community that is truly free, transcendent, becoming more human.

The attribute of language augments the attributes of material and human interaction. Language can express and bring into the open the thoughts and feelings of human beings. It can also hide and confound human thinking. Language can enlighten at the same time that it can obscure. Language can free. Language can enslave. Nevertheless, whether put to humane use or dehumanized purpose, language remains a distinct mark of humanity.[35]

Alienation

Macquarrie's discussion of human attributes has been to this point much more than a collection of sundry characteristics. Not only does he present the attributes as interdependent, with a whole greater than the sum of the parts, but he also presents these human attributes in view of their limits and negations.

Death has already been mentioned as the supreme limit of human becoming and will be considered in greater detail below. Death, however, is foreshadowed by the attribute of alienation. More than any other attribute in Macquarrie's list of human attributes, alienation is present in all the attributes of human experience.

> Alienation arises as an aspect or structure of man's "falling;" in his concern with and absorption in the world of things [this also includes the world of interpersonal human contacts], man falls away from the possibilities of a genuine personal being. He becomes alienated or estranged from his true self.[36]

One could say that he "dies." It will be considered below how the overcoming of alienation is directly related to any transcending of death.

The alienation that arises in each attribute discussed thus far plays a significant role in the process of becoming. Alienation, while sounding a negative tone, is the catalyst preventing any static state of being from continuing in humanity. In the attribute of freedom, alienation creates the twin poles of creative, life-enhancing exhilaration in the face of freedom, or the dreadful anxiety and great fear that seizes the human being in his freedom.[37] In the attribute of transcendence alienation creates the "other" toward which one moves to become more, or away from which one moves in a subhuman direction.[38] In the attribute of embodiedness, alienation can turn body and soul against each other or serve to enhance the connections between the two.[39]

A similar comparison can be traced through all the attributes discussed so far. Indeed, Macquarrie demonstrates for each attribute how alienation is the catalyst for becoming more human, or, tragically, becoming less human. "The word 'alienation' in its most basic sense means either the process of becoming other, or the state of having become other."[40] This becoming or having become other can be neutral—simply more other than previously—or it can be negative—being other than one ought to be.[41] In either case there is something of an either/or where something else dies, that is, there is now a breach between the former and latter. In alienation either the human becomes more human and the former existence dies, is left behind, or the human becomes less human and the transcendent other dies. Thus, harkening back to the first and prime attribute of freedom, alienation, like death, can become the means to destroy freedom. It is fatalism in its purest form—alienation from everything, with no potential in any direction.

Is there a transcending of alienation? Since Macquarrie has posited alienation as an attribute of human beings,[42] transcending alienation would be to transcend humanity itself. Is humanity itself a horizon to be transcended? The answer is yet to be considered.

The Ethical and Play

The remaining ethical attributes impinging upon the attribute of alienation are conscience, commitment, belief and love. In one sense these attributes begin to transcend alienation, and so transcend humanity. Conscience is the listening to a dynamic call versus listening to the voice of conventional wisdom.[43] It is much akin to Nietzsche's *Übermensch* whose will overcomes the weakness of those consumed by alienation.[44] Nietzsche, contemptuous of conventional morality, called human beings to an undefined—undefined by him—new morality.[45] Macquarrie sees in this Jesus' own call to a new morality, undefined by rules but open to the freedom of his followers' faith.[46] However, Nietzsche is too individualistic for Macquarrie, yet an appeal to public conscience is too undependable. For Macquarrie then, it is not will in a vacuum—individual or societal—but will in concert with the attributes of commitment, belief and love. It is not will curved in upon itself but a will transcending self, creating a true self in the transcending.[47]

For Macquarrie, a healthy amount of play balances the ethical attributes of humanity. He looks to his own upbringing in Scottish Protestantism and its serious work ethic as an example of imbalance. "I have never lost my respect for the busy bee, but in course of time I have come to prefer butterflies."[48] The human being needs leisure and relaxation as much as work. Art comes to be, then, the mingling of play with the deeper aspects of human nature. "In its simplest forms, art is scarcely distinguishable from play."[49] In its sophisticated forms art carries the inexpressible into new ways of expression.

In a secularized world art becomes a substitute for religion for some people. Macquarrie finds in this substitution a reflection of play. Religion is that attribute of humanity that gives a measure of joy into the severity of human nature. Here there is a tension as in the other attributes. One type of religion in humanity rises out of the seriousness of the limits and failures of human transcendence. The other kind of religion rises out of the desire to pursue potentialities that spring from the crossing of horizons in the human becoming. These types can sometimes be found together in the same religion. In Christianity, for example, Martin Luther like St. Paul exemplifies the former. Experiences of dramatic conflict and conversion in times of guilt or despair move them to assurances of salvation. John, the beloved disciple, exemplifies the latter, the fulfilling of a natural drive towards God without any violent conversion or overturning of a former way of life. "The two types of religious experiences seem to alternate...at different times."[50] For Macquarrie, these two are not mutually exclusive, but rather are binary components revolving around each other.[51] Whether violent or irenic, religious experience is integral to human becoming.

Austerity

Macquarrie describes the last three attributes to be discussed "austere"—suffering, death and hope. Does humanity need to suffer? A superficial, materialist-oriented perspective of personal peace and prosperity would deny a place to the attribute of suffering. A transcending humanity, from such a point of view, would see suffering as a horizon to be avoided. Macquarrie suggests instead that humanity view suffering as an attribute which insures the continuing of the transcendence of humanity.[52] Not an avoidance of suffering, but an embracing of the potential that comes from suffering is the key to human becoming.

However far humanity may transcend in its becoming, it never escapes the constraint of nature called death. Death and dying— whether anticipation of one's own death or the death of another—colors human existence more than anything else with a sense of finitude. Death presents a strong contrast. On the one hand it is the final limit a human being cannot cross. Thus it plays the role of giving structure to all that precedes it.[53] Yet, hope is an attribute that would pass over the horizon of death.

Macquarrie prefers to speak of a "hope beyond death" rather than a "life after death."[54] Death becomes then both limit and attribute— hinted at by the same dual nature of alienation—impelling the transcending human being toward something more in hope. Death does not erase the attributes of freedom, embodiedness, cognition, love, play, etc, but influences them as they influence it. There is in death a sign of something else—Being.

"It is only through confrontation with the nothing [of death] that for the first time we become seized of the wonder of Being."[55] This statement by Heidegger reflects Macquarrie's view of death.[56] Being is desired and obtained when humanity appreciates the finitude of death. Is Being rightly understood by Christians as God? Can Being be brought to light in the attributes of humanity bound by the attribute of death? The next section of this chapter will present Macquarrie's answers to these questions. With the third section of this chapter, on Christology, the discussion will show how Being is obtained in and by humanity.

III. The Presence of Divinity

A Something More in Humanity

In each of the attributes of humanity discussed in the preceding section there has been an implication for considering something more than humanity. That something more is God. "Every entity, as something that *is*, is a bearer of or a participant in Being. It can therefore function as a symbol of Being."[57] Throughout his book, *In Search of Humanity*, Macquarrie considers divinity to be reflected in humanity. This section will now consider the human attributes again, but this time as reflecting divinity. "The business of philosophical theology...is to bring these assumptions out into the open, to express them in a precise philosophical language (so far as this may be possible), and then to subject them to scrutiny to see whether they can stand up."[58]

In the course of this section on the presence of divinity in the human attributes, criticism of Macquarrie's explication also will be considered as a means to further clarify the divine potential in the human attributes. In the discussion of the fundamental human attributes—freedom, transcendence, egoity and embodiedness—Macquarrie quickly meets a challenge in God, traditionally understood, and in God as reflected in these first attributes. "The problem is whether human freedom is compatible with the existence of God."[59] This challenge is based on a critical assumption that if God exists, he has already determined what now is to become. And if God has determined what now is to become, then there is no freedom for humanity to become what it chooses. The conflict between freewill and determinism appears irreconcilable.

Macquarrie suggests that instead of considering God as the enemy of freedom, God is the benefactor and protector of human freedom. The human attribute to create possibility out of nothing is seen by Macquarrie as a sign of God in humanity. Traditional natural theology sees traces of the presence of God in what has been created. Macquarrie posits a sign of God's presence in what he has left uncreated—human potentiality in freedom.

This inference drawn from human freedom affects the traditional understanding of the *imago Dei* in humanity. Rather than some static quality of the residual creative action of God left in humanity, Macquarrie suggests that the image of God in humanity is the human share in the mystery of creating. It is human freedom and divine creativity in concert rather than in conflict.[60] The discussion of transcendence brings this further to light. Transcendence in humanity was shown to be that attribute of creative freedom that leads to a becoming something more. It was seen to be a qualitative something more rather than quantitative. Now traditionally speaking, transcendence has been applied to God rather than humanity. God as transcendent over creation is a wholly other. But if God were only wholly other, there would be nothing in the way of reflection in humanity of this wholly other God. Yet on the other hand, an immanent God would be so wholly within creation that there would be no sign of a something else, a something more in humanity. Thus rather than reserving the traits of transcendence and immanence to God alone, Macquarrie applies them both to God and humanity.

Transcendence in humanity has God as the goal of human transcendence.

> Human transcendence [reaches] the point at which human life has become so closely united with the divine life that, in traditional language, it has been 'deified.' It has not, however, ceased to be human—rather, for the first time, we learn what true humanity is.[61]

It is the doctrine of *theosis*, where a human being in freedom becomes something more, that is, becomes a participant in the life of God.[62] Human transcendence is the becoming toward a goal, the realm that lies outside the limits of humanity's possibilities.[63] On the other hand, Macquarrie appreciates the atheistic philosophers who hold that divine transcendence is a barrier to human transcendence. For these philosophers, God cannot be the goal of humanity; God is opposed to human transcendence.

While "God as goal" and "God as barrier" in human transcendence implies a contradiction, Macquarrie outlines an alternative solution. His solution places both God and humanity in dynamic terms. Rather than considering God as the static goal of a dynamic, transcending humanity, both God and humanity are becoming something more. In this way God becomes "non-oppressive" toward human transcendence. A non-oppressive conception

> would mean an understanding of divine transcendence that could be seen as liberating and encouraging *vis à vis* human transcending, rather than as the ultimate control that has already settled everything in advance, including the very goal of man's transcending freedom.[64]

Humanity has a capacity to become more than itself. God has a capacity to move beyond himself towards new goals. This is the sort of human and divine transcendence reflected in the attribute of human transcendence.

Critique of Macquarrie's Anthropological Method

David Jenkins, in a thorough analysis of Macquarrie's methodology, finds much to compliment but in the end is critical. "Phenomenology [Jenkins' term for Macquarrie's method] is not in itself, however, sufficient for satisfying our desire to grasp the deeper meaning of the phenomena that present themselves in human experience."[65]   Jenkins sees Macquarrie's phenomenology in the Schleiermacherian sense, that is, the interpretation of the phenomena is found in the subjective experience of the beholder of the phenomena.   According to such a view, then, Macquarrie does not put sufficient emphasis on the facts, putting emphasis instead on the meaning of the facts perceived in the experience of humanity.   He criticizes Macquarrie for not sufficiently balancing human becoming with that which is given.   Macquarrie's method, Jenkins concludes, is too dynamic, too dependent on subjective human experience, for the static nature of Christian doctrine.[66]   "We have noted that Macquarrie has an ambiguous relationship to whatever we might call facts.   He is ready enough to deal with the scientific, factual domain as a phenomenologist...but this leaves the notion of scientific truth, or empirical truth, unclarified."[67]

Macquarrie himself, however, accepts the label of phenomenology but not in the Schleiermacherian sense.   Macquarrie finds Tillich's thought in keeping with his own:

> The test of a phenomenological description is that the picture given by it is convincing, that it can be seen by anyone who is willing to look in the same direction, that the description illuminates other related ideas, and that it makes the reality these ideas are meant to reflect understandable.[68]

Convincing, publicly accessible, inter-related, leading to a better understanding of the reality of the experience—these are the strong points of phenomenology as Macquarrie accepts it for his purpose. Macquarrie's method is not an imprecise way of speaking, as Jenkins charges, but it has utmost concern for greater precision.

Macquarrie finds more fruitful the consideration of what is not known, not given, but what is perceived in the manner described above. He sees more *truth* in the *larvae Dei*, the "masks of God," worn in the attributes of humanity. It is an approach to God from his backside. "For no one may see my face and live." (Exodus 33:20) What is true in the mask of God called freedom, transcendence, etc, in humanity is not a static, given nature. Rather the truth is shown in reference to the becoming of humanity and God in freedom. As stated earlier, Macquarrie does not reject empirical knowledge. He considers it insufficient. There is something more beyond to which the facts are sign posts.

However, the sign posts are not incidental to the becoming. The *larvae Dei* in human attributes are not *outer* signs of *inner* truth. The human attributes are not *lower* qualities pointing to *higher* Being. Again there is in Macquarrie no desire to maintain such Augustinian distinctions, clothing a static being in dynamic attire. Macquarrie's signs, *contra* Jenkins, are not mere signs. Rather they are signs of what they signify. Human being and divine Being wear the same masks. Human being and divine Being bear the same attributes.

A Yet Something More

Macquarrie's purpose in explicating the attributes of humanity is to arrive at an anthropological argument for the existence of God.[69] As has been stated before, the consideration of these attributes cumulatively leads to a realization that there is a transhuman spiritual source. This becomes the subject of Macquarrie's second book in his trilogy, *In Search of Deity*. Only enough of this discussion will be presented here to introduce the final section on Christology where the transcending humanity and transcending deity meet.

Of the four fundamental attributes—freedom and transcendence having already been discussed above—embodiedness presents a special challenge as a sign of God. Embodiedness would seem to be the epitome of what God is not. Out of nothingness human freedom transcends the nothingness, a sign of divine transcendence, so out of embodiedness something more transcends. Embodiedness is a sign to the resurrection of the human body and the incarnation of the divine Being.[70] This is another thread to be woven into the Christological discussion to follow.

In Macquarrie's second set of attributes the presence of a divine sign is important. Human language is not simply idle talk or expression of static propositions about things; rather, language in human beings can be revelatory. "In what is most proper to it, [language] is a saying *of* that which reveals itself to human beings in manifold ways."[71] This is a sign of the language of God which speaks not propositional truth, but a creative/revelatory word.

The attributes relating to the material and interpersonal worlds—having and sociality— provide further signs of God. The tension of having/not having material goods and the confusion between materialism and asceticism signify having that transcends human having. God is the creator. Things belong ultimately to God. The social interactions of human beings signify God's interpersonal nature: both toward human beings and in the interaction among the persons of the Trinity. God "is the consummation of both individual and social existence, or, better expressed, he perfectly unites these two poles of personal existence."[72] Having/not having and individual/community are both a set of poles implying a fullness in God.

Enough has been said to demonstrate how Macquarrie sees human attributes as *symbols for Being*, the "aspects of human life...cumulatively directing us to a spiritual reality which is at once the source, support and goal of humanity."[73] Yet even the attributes which might be called *higher* (attributes which portray a more truly becoming human) —conscience, love, play, hope, etc—do not lead necessarily to greater self-knowledge. For Macquarrie the same difficulty of knowing oneself applies even more to assertions about the divine signs in humanity. "It should be the easiest [to acquire self-knowledge], for nothing is closer to man than himself; yet because of this very closeness, such knowledge can never be a matter of indifference or an abstract theoretical knowledge, and so what is closest in existence may be furthest in understanding."[74]

Not only is the knowing of humanity as human an elusive knowledge, but also, since the transcending God is signified by humanity, the becoming of God and the becoming of humanity toward something more remains elusive if not entirely incomprehensible. The closer humanity and God are understood to become, the more *wholly other* they remain. This paradoxical horizon is crossed in Jesus the Christ.

IV. Christology — A Becoming Together

"Christianity proclaims not an idealized possibility of existence but the appearance of the ideal in history."[75]   All talk about human possibility and potential, reflected in the various attributes that humanity has displayed in its history of becoming remains implication and inference outside of the occurrence in *a* human being in history, *in toto*. John Macquarrie's Christology collects the many anthropological strands discussed above and considers them in view of the man Jesus of Nazareth.   His final book of the trilogy, *Jesus Christ in Modern Thought*, completes the prolegomena introduced by anthropology and theology.

For Macquarrie, several issues must be considered in Christology. First, there is the historical issue.   How much historical data is necessary to demonstrate that the ideal of human potential has been realized in one person? Macquarrie views the Gospels as containing the meaning of Jesus of Nazareth, not merely biographical facts. He does not deny the place of such historical facts; but sees in them something more. Far from ignoring historical facts, Macquarrie holds that a person in the late twentieth century can know more about Jesus of Nazareth than that he lived and died.[76]

A historically significant issue is whether Jesus was conscious of his messianic identity.   While Macquarrie suggests that the Gospels record a "becoming" in Jesus' consciousness, Macquarrie also concludes that Jesus did become conscious and cognitively committed at some point, freely choosing the vocation that progressed even to the point of his death.[77] As to his understanding of his death, the events recorded by the New Testament evangelists support both Jesus' hope that he would accomplish his vocation without death, as well as his willingness to accept death if necessary with the understanding of something more to come from it.[78]

While critical scholarship questions much historical material once accepted as a given, Macquarrie does not ignore the historical issues. "Some minimum of factual history is needed in Christian theology."[79] It is needed to show the attributes of true humanity and true divinity actualized in time and not isolated in abstraction.

Two related issues in Christology besides the historical questions are the humanity of Jesus and his divinity. For if Jesus is the symbol of a truly complete humanity, what is his relation to humanity in general? Conversely, if he is the human symbol of divinity, what is his relationship to God?

Regarding humanity, Jesus differs in degree, not kind from humanity in general.[80] While emphasizing continuously Jesus' full humanity, Macquarrie insists that in Jesus something more is present. That vestige of the infinite called the sign of God as seen in human attributes has become more than vestige in Jesus.

> To call [Jesus] the God-man (or whatever the preferred expression may be] is to claim that in him human transcendence has reached that point at which the human life has become so closely united with the divine life that, in traditional language, it has been 'deified.' It has not, however, ceased to be human—rather, for the first time, we learn what true humanity is.[81]

In Jesus the realization of the divine signs has become the something more.

Is Jesus then the *Übermensch*, the human beyond which there can be no *more*? Is Jesus Nietzsche's fully autonomous human being? Again, while Macquarrie is sympathetic to Nietzsche's arguments, Macquarrie is not advocating an idealized human state. The man Jesus is not the goal toward which humanity moves. "We recognize him as the fulfillment of human experience, yet different from us in having brought the most central possibilities of humanity to a new level of realization."[82] A new level, but it is not the final level. For in Macquarrie's Christology Jesus remains the representative, *exemplum*, not the sole human being, *exemplar*.[83]

In the anthropological discussion above, that horizon beyond which it appears impossible for humanity to cross was introduced regarding human embodiedness and death. Christologically speaking this question arises: Is there something more to becoming fully human? Ancient Christian theologians spoke of the deification of humanity. This doctrine, however, still understood deification as a goal, an attainment of God's intention for humanity. In Jesus, however, the humanity has become something more. In Jesus God has transcended the horizon of humanity and entered that life.

Incarnation, the enfleshment of God, in the man Jesus would become a myth if a static understanding of God and humanity were maintained.[84] Myth can be a slippery term, as Macquarrie has often cautioned.[85]   Used here to define the static understanding of God and humanity, myth is a metaphorical story for a theological point. For Macquarrie, however, incarnation is not metaphorical.   It is anthropological.

Macquarrie's preference for the term "Christ-event" demonstrates his dynamic understanding of the incarnation.   "There is no sharp dividing line between Jesus and the community [of Christians]."[86] Thus the incarnation envelops the person of Jesus together with the human beings of the Christian community. Jesus, as the enfleshment of God becomes myth when he is isolated in himself. In the context of the Christian community, however, the enfleshment of God in both Jesus and humanity becomes a difference of degree, not kind; an incarnation of dynamic understanding, not mythological.[87] This is the attribute of transcendence noted earlier, which holds that Jesus is the meeting point between a transcending humanity and a transcending deity.

It is this meeting point in Jesus of a transcending humanity and a transcending deity which, for Macquarrie, sees the mask of God become the face of God. The possibility ("mask") that the human being is a being-in-transcendence with the capacity for manifesting the divine life becomes the actuality ("face") in Jesus Christ.[88] His emphasis on the signs of the divine in the human attributes is fulfilled in Jesus. For Macquarrie, only if there is already a possibility for transcendence and a capacity for God within all human beings—and his discussions of attributes concluded that there is such a possibility and capacity—can there be such a possibility and capacity in the man Jesus. At the same time, only if God makes himself present and known in and through creation in general—and the human attributes show this as well—can there be a particular point where he is present and known in a singular way.[89]   In Jesus universal humanity and divinity is combined with historical particularity, both human and divine.

However, Macquarrie does not assert that Jesus is unique. There is a difference in degree, not in kind. Jesus is the representative of humanity to divinity, of divinity to humanity. He is not a substitute for God or for humanity.   "A representative steps in for us, like the substitute, but unlike the substitute the representative holds the place open so that we can step in ourselves."[90]   With both a transcending humanity and a transcending divinity Jesus the representative holds open the place for both. His historical particularity is the potential for humanity to be with divinity. His divine particularity is the potential for divinity to be with humanity.

Like his anthropology, Macquarrie's Christology has generated criticism.   David Jenkins' criticism of Macquarrie's Christology is similar to his critique of Macquarrie's anthropology.   He finds Macquarrie ambiguous in his treatment of historical material.   Jenkins questions Macquarrie's discussion of the acts of Jesus as "events." "Facts seem to disappear altogether in favour of an existential-ontological interpretation of so-called 'events.'"[91]   Furthermore, Jenkins considers Macquarrie's modes of expression to be incomplete. For Jenkins, God and humanity do remain wholly others.   Jenkins cannot find sufficient support in Macquarrie for Macquarrie to hold both the otherness of God and humanity, as well as a denial of an absolute difference of kind between God and humanity.[92]

Another critic of Macquarrie's Christology is Charles Hefling. He acknowledges Macquarrie's claim to an *exemplum* in Jesus rather than *exemplar*, but faults Macquarrie for not holding true to his own argument.   "What it means to say [in Macquarrie's book] either of Jesus' identity or of his activity that divinity has entered into it turns out to be very elusive."[93]   Hefling grants that there may indeed be "signs" of the divine in humanity, even in Jesus.   Yet he sees in Macquarrie a remaining distinction of kind not degree in how the transcending from below of humanity meets the transcending from above of divinity in the man Jesus. Hefling faults Macquarrie for being imprecise.[94]

Both Jenkins and Hefling criticize Macquarrie for imprecision. As has been shown above in the presentation of Macquarrie's anthropology and Christology—and especially in Macquarrie's discussion of a narrow empiricism—Macquarrie is intent upon capturing the peculiarities of theological language.   The fault is not that Macquarrie is imprecise. Rather, the fault lies with the critics, Jenkins and Hefling, who expect language about becoming, potentiality and possibility to be explicated in static terms. As Macquarrie says of language, "Language is not static but keeps growing and deepening.   It does not just describe things as they are, but...opens up new levels of awareness."[95]

V. Death Transcended, Transcending

The death of Jesus on the cross is the most comprehensive event in Macquarrie's Christology.   Therefore, consideration of Macquarrie's understanding of Jesus' death will serve to conclude this chapter.

As noted earlier, Macquarrie writes, "I believe that to some extent God's image remains vestigially in every human being, but the Christian claim is that in Jesus Christ that image has clearly shown forth."[96] Macquarrie's *credo* maintains the continuity of image both in God and in humanity manifested in Jesus Christ. This image is viewed most clearly through Jesus Christ crucified. Since the clear image is one of suffering and death on the cross, what does it say for God's own image and God's vestigial image in humanity? These are the questions that revolve around the event of the cross.

Macquarrie wrestles with the place of suffering and death as attributes of humanity. He finds a connection between the suffering and death of human beings and the suffering and death of Jesus. However, Macquarrie eschews a connection that would rely upon substitute imagery. "A substitute stands in and does something for us, in our place. We remain passive while the substitute gets on with it—indeed we would not even need to know that he had done anything at all."[97]

Macquarrie rejects this kind of substitutionary language as a description for what happens with Jesus. He rejects it because "the understanding of God [is] a highly questionable one...the understanding of salvation is a poor one."[98] The whole discussion speaks only of punishment and its escape. For Macquarrie the preferred view is a "representative" view of what Jesus has done. "The representative also steps in for us [as does the substitute], but he holds the place open for us so that we can step in ourselves. The Christian must consciously appropriate the work of Christ on his or her behalf, and take up the cross."[99] Substitutionary language leaves the suffering and dying Christian atoned, yet the Christian still suffers and dies. The representative understanding claims more. The word "representative" itself implies a connection between the representative and the one represented. But is this connection only that of an *exemplar* as Macquarrie's critics assert? Or is it an *exemplum et sacramentum* relationship? Or is it something altogether different?

Consideration of these questions leads Macquarrie to begin with the human being who suffers.[100] Macquarrie seeks to avoid answering these questions in terms of a God who rescues the sufferer from troubles because that could lead to a substitutionary understanding of Jesus' death. Furthermore, to talk of God's role in human suffering is to turn to speculation, to something further removed from human beings

who suffer and die. "We live in a secular age, where the very word
'God' has become elusive for many people. How then can we hope to
speak intelligibly of Jesus Christ if one begins by talking about his
coming from God and identifying him with the divine Logos?"[101]
"Logos," "Word," elude any identification with the human predicament.
According to Macquarrie, for the everyday sort of person, "God" is the
"wholly other," the one who is unlike us.   How can God or Word
suffer and die like us?

   Therefore, to formulate an answer to human suffering and death,
Macquarrie begins, not "above" with God, but "below" with Jesus.
Jesus is a man who suffers and dies. Yet perhaps he is also the Man
who suffers and dies.[102] "The Man" means that in Jesus there is more
than simply "a man."   Indeed, beginning to answer questions about
human suffering and death by beginning with Jesus' suffering and death
leads one to some startling answers. To "begin from the humanity of
Christ is not to decide in advance that it cannot go any further."[103]
   In this way, Macquarrie echoes Martin Luther.[104] Luther wrote,

> The Scriptures begin very gently, and lead us to Christ as to a man,
> and then to the one who is Lord over all creatures, and after that to
> one who is God... But the philosophers and doctors have insisted on
> beginning from above. We begin from below, and after that move
> upwards.[105]

   This "from below" starting point leads Macquarrie to suggest two
endings to the life of Jesus.   Macquarrie calls them "The Happy
Ending" and "The Austere Ending."[106]   Both endings are intended to
outline the aftermath of Jesus' death. The "Happy Ending" follows the
death of Jesus with the descent into hell, the resurrection, the ascension
and the second coming. This ending "is supported by the majority of
New Testament writers, it is incorporated into the catholic creeds, and
it is re-enacted year by year in the liturgical calendar of the
church."[107]

   While the "Happy Ending" "*deserves* to be true"[108] Macquarrie is
compelled to consider the alternative. The "Austere Ending" finishes
with Jesus' death on the cross. The "joyful mysteries" of the "Happy
Ending" are omitted.   Following the Gospel of John, however,
Macquarrie points to the paradox of Jesus' death. "Jesus exaltation *is*
the cross!   His exaltation *is* his humiliation!"[109]   In this way
Macquarrie places the resurrection in the dynamic of the cross.

Resurrection is an event, like the incarnation discussed above, that begins in Jesus but is at the same an event in the life of the church.[110]

Thus while it is important for Macquarrie to say that Jesus is a man, a human being, there is that sense that because Jesus is "Jesus" there is something more about him. This something more is that "perhaps he is the Man, the archetype of humanity."[111] The suggestion is that this man, this probable archetype, shares in human suffering and death while also leading to the "something more" implied in his person.

The humanness of Jesus is a humanness that must be complete even to the point of suffering and death, for suffering and death are part of the human experience. Yet too often it is precisely in Jesus' suffering and death that the divine is put forth so as to hinder this man from being a man in human fullness.

The classical Christologies, which assume an impassibility of the divine nature must wrestle with how to explain Jesus' death and yet keep him fully divine. Such a Christology that begins "from above," that is busy trying to answer the divine questions, has a formidable obstacle in Jesus' death.

> The traditional teaching does not give any satisfactory answer to the question, 'How is it possible for this person, Jesus Christ, to have a vital significance or a saving significance for human beings living many centuries after his time in different parts of the planet?'"[112]

Not only is "a vital significance" for living humanity difficult, but more so, Macquarrie implies that it is difficult for there to be any "vital significance" for dying humanity.

Macquarrie's Jesus is fully human. He dies. Macquarrie prefers not even to ease Jesus' dying by quickly moving on to the state of exaltation following death, Macquarrie's so-called "Happy Ending" to the events of the life of Jesus.[113] He has a more "austere" desire.

> The need to be absolutely honest compels us to look at an alternative scenario. Suppose in our account of the career of Jesus we had felt compelled to draw the bottom line under the cross? Suppose we omitted the 'joyful mysteries' that traditionally come after the cross?[114]

In other words, what if Jesus the man, even Jesus the archetype human, died, period? Jesus' humanity is so complete, that, like all human beings, his death is final. This is a thought "so austere we naturally shrink from it."[115]

It is common to speak of Jesus' resurrection along with his death. "The crucified and risen Lord" is the phrase often used. The "...and risen" comes so quickly, perhaps too thoughtlessly. Resurrection is not something human beings can know. "[Resurrection] eludes our understanding so long as we are seeing it only from below."[116] We can know only death. Therefore, Macquarrie states that Jesus' death is the full extent of Jesus' humanity. He is truly *consubstantial* with human flesh and blood, *consubstantial* with human suffering, *consubstantial* with human death.[117]

There is now a startling "something more" to be considered in the Jesus who dies. Macquarrie's discussion implies the doctrine that has come to be called the *communicatio idiomatum*, "communication of attributes." This doctrine describes the mutual predication of human and divine attributes in Jesus Christ.[118]

Macquarrie turns away from a Platonic idea of an immutable and impassible God. Though he does not use the doctrinal term, *genus tapeinotikon*, Macquarrie does push the sharing of attributes to its fullest extent as a completely mutual sharing.[119] It is the full extent of the incarnation.

> As we ourselves move toward a more dynamic conception of God and think of him not as dwelling in a distant heaven in untroubled bliss but as transcending in the sense of constantly coming forth from himself, then the idea of incarnation [in both embodiedment and the death of the embodied] will not seem to be some improbable speculation or some fragment of a fantastic mythology.[120]

This thorough sharing of attributes leads Macquarrie to rescue the impassibility of God from Platonism and give it a more Christian understanding.

> I would prefer to call it the 'serenity' of God, and by that I mean that to God there belongs a deep serenity that can never be overwhelmed, so that he is able to accept and to absorb and even transmute into good all the sufferings of his creatures. It is not that he is untouched by these sufferings, but that he has the power and capacity to take

them to himself and not be destroyed by them.[121]

This is a dynamic understanding of impassability rather than a static understanding. While Macquarrie does not say "God dies," yet the suffering that can lead to destruction certainly implies death. But God "has the infinite capacity to bear"[122] even death. Thus, not only does the man Jesus share humanity in its fullness unto death, but the God-in-man Jesus also shares humanity to its fullest depth in death.

In his "Austere Ending" to the mysteries of Jesus Christ[123] Macquarrie questions his conclusion that Jesus' death was the final event of his humanity. "Have I...been selling out completely to modern secular thought, to which ideas like resurrection and ascension are myths, not to be taken seriously? No..."[124] Macquarrie has stated that,

> If the highest virtue is the kind of love which the New Testament attributes to Jesus ["No greater love has anyone than this, that he lay down his life for his friends."], then it seems to me that his victory over evil was already won in the agonizing hour before his death, and that it would remain decisive even if there were no subsequent events of resurrection and ascension..."[125]

Macquarrie's "even if" requires explication.

He points to Jesus' own words in the Gospel of John about the cross. "'I, when I am lifted up from the earth, will draw all men to myself.' He said this to show by what death he was to die." (John 12:32-33) As mentioned above, Macquarrie comments, "Of all the Johannine paradoxes, this one is surely the most striking. Jesus' exaltation is the cross! His exaltation is his humiliation!"[126] Jesus is his most fully human, his most fully archetypal, in his weakest moment—suffering and death.

Macquarrie's understanding of the cross as exaltation can lead the Christian to recognize that in his or her suffering Jesus is there. The Lord Jesus suffers and dies. God suffers and dies. In this way, suffering and death are changed. They are changed because of the one who enters into them. If a human being dies, a human being dies. If Jesus dies, a man dies. But when Jesus the Man dies, when God dies, something happens to death. Death dies.[127] This is all very "austere," but already there is a sense of something more, a transcending.

In his discussion concerning the divinity of Jesus Christ, Macquarrie states,

> In our exposition, we have given priority to deification, the raising of
> a man toward God for it has seemed necessary to maintain the full
> and utter humanity of Christ against all the tendencies that would turn
> him into an alien supernatural being. But we have never denied that
> finally we must come to terms with Paul's assertion that 'all this is
> from God' and that the raising of a human life to the level at which
> it manifested God is possible only through the descent of God into
> that life.[128]

There is a both/and for Macquarrie—human *deification*, humanity
participating in the divine life, and divine *inhumanization*, God
participating in the human life, belong together.[129]   This is
Macquarrie's understanding of the cross. The cross is the focus, the
meeting of human *deification* and divine *inhumanization*. On the cross
a man, the Man, the God-in-man, dies.   God dies.   Yet in this
humiliation on the cross there is "the possession and mediation...of true
life, eternal life."[130]

God on the cross has come "out of his transcendence in a generous
overflow of love so as to identify with the world."[131]   It is an identity
so intimate as to die with the world. This transcending of God in death
meets on the cross a transcending of humanity in that death. It is a
transcending that moves beyond death to life.

But if death dies, how can it become life? If a transcending God
dies, does not everything perish? Macquarrie concludes his discussion
of the austerity of Jesus' death by saying

> I leave to the reader the choice between Ending A [the traditional
> resurrection, ascension ending] and Ending B [the austere, 'Jesus dies'
> ending]. Both, I think, can find roots in the scriptures, both conserve
> the essential truths of Christianity, both can find modern ways of
> being expressed, but I doubt if they can both be combined into an
> intelligible unity.[132]

Macquarrie himself, however, does set the stage for an intelligible
unity. His discussions about freedom and transcendence are set in a
discussion of the creation of the new out of nothing. The direction
toward which his whole discussion about the attributes of humanity as
signs of God's attributes and presence in humanity leads to the

something more, the something new in Jesus of Nazareth. By participation in Jesus Christ the old becomes new. Divine attributes become *inhumanized*; human attributes become *deified*. Thus, *mutatis mutandis*, it is true for the seemingly opposites of life and death.

As the Gospel of John records in chapter 11, perhaps as the evangelist's sermon on Jesus' own death, Jesus says to the grief-stricken Martha, "I am the resurrection and the life. He who believes in me will live, even though he dies..." (John 11:25) This is truly the case because Jesus has entered death, because God has died with dying humanity. "In dying we live" because in dying God continues to surpass himself beyond his dying.[133] Humanity that dies transcends death into life because the living God transcends life into death. This living and dying, this dying and living, come together in Jesus Christ. "Transcendence of humanity from below...is met by the divine transcendence from above."[134]

With Macquarrie's talk of transcendence—both human and divine—suffering and death are also something that happen to human beings, beginning at a particular point. Yet for Macquarrie, "a dynamic understanding of 'being' as including 'becoming' is a legitimate interpretation of the traditional way of speaking."[135] Suffering and death thus are part of "becoming," a something more. Furthermore, while it is of the nature of humanity to suffer and die, "nature" too has taken on new significance. "We move away from the static understanding of 'nature' as a fixed essence to the dynamic or processive understanding of *physis* as 'emergence' or 'coming into being.'"[136] In its very suffering and dying, human nature is "coming into being" in a very new way!

This is what the suffering and death of Jesus—the Man and the God-in-man—on the cross brings into focus. The cross is not simply a sign of what God is doing. The cross of Jesus "is the progressive presencing and self-manifestation of the Logos in the physical and historical world."[137] The death of Jesus on the cross is God become human and the human (representative man, as Macquarrie calls Jesus) become divine in its fullest sense, diminishing neither the human nor the divine, neither easing the austerity of suffering and death nor cheapening the transcending reality of eternal, new life.

It can be startling to discover that in suffering and death there is something new. However, this is Macquarrie's understanding of the cross. Human suffering and death in the light of the cross can bring about

> an experience of Jesus Christ in which we recognize him as the
> fulfillment of our humanity, one with us in the whole spectrum of
> human experience [especially the experience of death], yet different
> from us in having brought the most central possibilities of humanity
> to a new level of realization.[138]

"Dying we live" because now we die in and with Jesus Christ, through
whom we also live.   Once again Macquarrie views Christ as
"representative," not "substitute," Savior.

In an early disputation—the Heidelberg Disputation of
1518—Martin Luther penned a series of theses for debate. Two of
those theses are particularly important in this context. "He deserves to
be called a theologian, however, who comprehends the visible and
manifest things of God seen through suffering and the cross...A
theologian of glory calls evil good and good evil. A theologian of the
cross calls the thing what it really is."[139]

What the thing is is a becoming thing, a transcending thing.
Suffering and death have not changed their "thing-hood"—the evil is not
good. But what "actually is" is death transcended for humanity in and
with this Jesus Christ.   Through his anthropological Christology,
Macquarrie has "manifested the things of God" through the mask of
God become the face of God seen in human suffering and death.

> "True life in death" has brought us therefore to the central mysteries
> of the incarnation, the coming together in unity of God and
> man..."True life in death" sounds like nonsense, but according to the
> Christian religion, it is nothing other than God's mysterious destiny
> for our being...This is only what Christ himself is reported to have
> taught: "If any man would come after me, let him deny himself and
> take up his cross daily and follow me. For whoever would save his
> life will lose it; and whoever loses his life for my sake, he will save
> it."[140]

Notes

1. John Macquarrie, *Studies in Christian Existentialism* (London: SCM Press
Ltd., 1965), 96.

2. John Macquarrie, *In Search of Humanity* (New York: The Crossroad Publishing Co., 1983), 2.

3. Alister Kee & Eugene T. Long, editors, *Being and Truth: Essays in Honor of John Macquarrie* (London: SCM Press, Ltd., 1986), xvii.

4. Ibid., xviii.

5. Macquarrie, *In Search of Humanity*, 253.

6. Ibid., 254.

7. Macquarrie, contrary to Irenaeus and others who make a distinction between "image" (*imago*) and "likeness" (*similitudo*) as these are used in Genesis 1, follows the line of thought present from the Reformation onwards which does not make a distinction between "image" and "likeness." See pages 38-39 above for Macquarrie's related discussion of the process of divine *inhumanization* and human *deification*.

8. Macquarrie, *In Search of Humanity*, 14.

9. Ibid., 11.

10. The mystery of divine *fiat*, "Let there be," is experienced on a finite level by human beings in their exercise of freedom. "Out of nothing that is not yet determined, [human beings] bring forth something to which they have given a definite shape." (Macquarrie, *In Search of Humanity*, 13.) This will be discussed in greater detail in section *III*.

11. Macquarrie, *In Search of Humanity*, 26.

12. Ibid., 38-40.

13. Ibid., 38. The word *hegemonikon* is derived from the Greek verb *hegeisthai*, "to lead," and was used by the Stoic philosophers and some Church Fathers for what might be called the "leading edge" of a person, i.e., the conscious, rational element.

14. Ibid.

15. Ibid., 49-51.

16. Macquarrie, *In Search of Humanity*, 19.

17. Ibid., 19.

18. Ibid., 20-21.

19. The Old World certainty that nothing lay beyond the horizon (*ne plus ultra*) was shattered by Columbus' discovery of a new world beyond the known world. The Spanish royal family removed the negative from its motto to boldly declare *plus ultra*, "more beyond." This likewise is significantly related to the potentials of a "new world" beyond the present limits of embodied humanity.

20. Macquarrie, *Studies in Christian Existentialism*, 506. The subject of death is significant for Macquarrie, both in his anthropology and in his Christology. This subject will be discussed in greater detail in a later section.

21. Macquarrie, *In Search of Humanity*, 7.

22. The term "interactive," like that of "fundamental" in the previous section, for describing this set of attributes is my own conclusion based on inferences drawn from Macquarrie's discussions.

23. Macquarrie, *In Search of Humanity*, 59.

24. Ibid.

25. Ibid., 60-61.

26. Ibid., 67-68.

27. Ibid., 68.

28. Ibid.

29. Ibid. 83.

30. Ibid., 86.

31. Ibid., 87.

32. Ibid.

33. Macquarrie, *In Search of Humanity*, 88.

34. Ibid., 32.

35. Ibid., 96.

36. Macquarrie, *Studies in Christian Existentialism*, 132.

37. Macquarrie, *In Search of Humanity*, 21.

38. Ibid., 34-35.

39. Ibid., 58.

40. Ibid., 107.

41. Ibid., 108.

42. Ibid., Chapter *X*.

43. Ibid., 130.

44. The term *Übermensch*, "superman," is implied in the discussions of Macquarrie's book, *In Search of Humanity*, p. 131, but appropriated from Nietzsche in Macquarrie's *Jesus Christ in Modern Thought*, p. 365. In this latter reference Macquarrie writes, "Nietzsche's superman is a secularized and dechristianized version of the God-man."

45. Macquarrie, *In Search of Humanity*, 131.

46. Ibid.

47. Ibid., 142-143.

48. Ibid., 188.

49. Ibid., 192.

50. Ibid., 209.

51. Ibid., 210.

52. Macquarrie, *In Search of Humanity*, 229.

53. Ibid., 241.

54. Ibid., 252.

55. Macquarrie, *Studies in Christian Existentialism*, 88.

56. For Macquarrie's indebtedness to Heidegger's thought see also Macquarrie's translation of Martin Heidegger, *Being and Time* (New York: Harper & Row, 1962); also John Macquarrie, *An Existential Theology: A Comparison of Heidegger and Bultmann* (New York: Harper & Row, 1960) and John Macquarrie, *Studies in Christian Existentialism*.

57. Macquarrie, *Studies in Christian Existentialism*, 95.

58. John Macquarrie, *Principles of Christian Theology*, 2nd edition (New York: Charles Scribner's Sons, 1977), 36.

59. Macquarrie, *In Search of Humanity*, 15.

60. Ibid., 23-24.

61. John Macquarrie, *Jesus Christ in Modern Thought* (London: SCM Press, Ltd., 1990), 370.

62. In the New Testament, II Peter 1:4 speaks of Christians as those who "became partakers (κοινωνοὶ) of the divine nature." This "participation" in the divine nature receives further emphasis by Athanasius in his familiar dictum, "God became man that man might become divine." C.M. Allchin, *Participation in God* (Wilton, Connecticut: Morehouse-Barlow, 1988) traces this doctrine of *theosis* in the Anglican tradition beginning with Andrewes and Hooker, through Charles Wesley, Pusey and the Oxford Movement, and into the present. In Lutheran theology, Martin Luther received the theme of participation in the divine via the Christmas liturgy. The "joyous exchange" (*admirabile commercium*) became his expression, though Luther limits the exchange to sin and justification through faith in Christ. Cf. Martin Luther, "The Freedom of a Christian, 1520," *Luther's Works, Vol. 31* (Philadelphia: Fortress Press, 1957).

63. Macquarrie, *In Search of Humanity*, 36.

64. Ibid., 36.

65. David Jenkins, *The Scope and Limits of John Macquarrie's Existential Theology* (Stockholm: Almqvist & Wiksell International, 1987), 81.

66. Jenkins, *Scope and Limits*, 83.

67. Ibid., 118.

68. Macquarrie, *In Search of Humanity*, 217.

69. Ibid., 257.

70. Ibid., 70.

71. Ibid., 106.

72. Ibid., 86.

73. Ibid., 257.

74. Macquarrie, *Principles of Christian Theology*, 59.

75. Ibid., 307.

76. Macquarrie, *Jesus Christ in Modern Thought*, 358.

77. Ibid., 354.

78. Ibid., 357.

79. Ibid., 358.

80. Ibid., 359.

81. Ibid., 370.

82. Ibid., 373.

83. While the terms *exemplar* and *exemplum* are often interchangeable (and Macquarrie does not use either term directly), they are used here to distinguish between Jesus as the model in whom God is at work (*exemplar*) and Jesus as the model with whom the Christian participates (*exemplum*).

84. Macquarrie, *Jesus Christ in Modern Thought*, 380.

85. Michael Green, *The Truth of God Incarnate* (London: Hodder and Stoughton, 1977), 140-144.

86. Macquarrie, *Jesus Christ in Modern Thought*, 21.

87. Ibid., 21-22.

88. Ibid., 372.

89. Ibid., 381.

90. Ibid., 402.

91. Jenkins, *Scope and Limits*, 146.

92. Ibid., 148-149.

93. Charles C. Hefling, "Reviving Adamic Adoptionism: The Example of John Macquarrie," *Theological Studies* 52 (S 1991):489.

94. Ibid., 490.

95. Macquarrie, *In Search of Humanity*, 105.

96. Macquarrie, *Jesus Christ in Modern Thought*, 382.

97. Ibid., 401-402.

98. Ibid.

99. Ibid.

100. Ibid., Chapter 17.

101. Ibid., 343.

102. Ibid., 359.

103. Ibid., 343.

104. Macquarrie approvingly cites Martin Luther as a corrective to any docetic tendencies in Christology. (*See* Macquarrie, *Jesus Christ in Modern Thought,* 290.)

105. Quoted in: David P. Scaer, *Christology,* "Confessional Lutheran Dogmatics, Vol. VI" (Lake Mills, Iowa: Graphic Publishing Co., Inc., 1989), 9.

106. Macquarrie, *Jesus Christ in Modern Thought,* 403-414.

107. Ibid., 463.

108. Ibid., 412.

109. Ibid., 413.

110. Ibid., 414.

111. Ibid., 360.

112. Ibid., 315.

113. Ibid., 403-411.

114. Ibid., 412.

115. Ibid.

116. Ibid., 409.

117. Ibid., 363.

118. The communication of attributes (*communicatio idiomatum*) relates to the personal union of the God-man (*unio personalis*). If the Son of God is not merely a phantasm but a real man, then with his humanity he has a whole set of human attributes. Conversely, if the Son of Man is God not merely in name but truly God, then the Son of Man possess with the divine nature the whole set of divine attributes. In Lutheran theology this doctrine of the communication of attributes can be further explicated under three *genera: genus idiomaticum,* the appropriation of attributes by the two natures; *genus maiestaticum,* the communication of majesty to the human nature; *genus apotelesmaticum,* the communication of official acts between the two natures.

119. The *genus tapeinotikon* is a corresponding term to the *genus maiestaticum*. The *genus tapeinotikon* is the communication of human attributes to the divine nature in Jesus, the God-man. For a thorough discussion of this *genus* and its implications for Luther's *theologia crucis* see Marc Lienhard, *Luther: Witness to Jesus Christ* (Minneapolis: Augsburg Publishing House, 1982), 339-341, 344-345. There is a great similarity between Luther's thought and Macquarrie's thought in this area.

120. Macquarrie, *Jesus Christ in Modern Thought*, 380.

121. John Macquarrie, *The Humility of God* (London: SCM Press, Ltd., 1978), 69.

122. Ibid.

123. Macquarrie, *Jesus Christ in Modern Thought*, 412-414.

124. Ibid., 413.

125. Ibid., 412.

126. Ibid., 413.

127. Cf. Romans 5 or II Timothy 1:10.

128. Macquarrie, *Jesus Christ in Modern Thought*, 375-376.

129. Macquarrie suggests that the early Church might have been wiser to use the Greek term *enanthropoesis*, "inhumanization," instead of "incarnation" as a corresponding term to *theopoiesis/theosis*, "deification." Cf. Macquarrie, *Jesus Christ in Modern Thought*, 116-117, 375.

130. Macquarrie, *Jesus Christ in Modern Thought*, 414.

131. Ibid., 380.

132. Ibid., 414.

133. Ibid., 379-381.

134. Ibid., 380.

135. Macquarrie, *Jesus Christ in Modern Thought*, 384.

136. Ibid., 385.

137. Ibid., 392.

138. Ibid., 373.

139. Martin Luther, "Heidelberg Disputation," *Luther's Works, Volume 31* (Philadelphia: Fortress Press, 1957), 53.

140. Macquarrie, *Studies in Christian Existentialism*, 243-245.

Chapter 3

Wolfhart Pannenberg

I. Introduction

The writings of Wolfhart Pannenberg have the distinct characteristic that their complexity sometimes can be expressed by the theologian in deceptively simple terms. In reality the very simplicity of some of Pannenberg's Christological and anthropological statements carries profound implications. For the purpose of this chapter Pannenberg's illustration of a flower serves perfectly. "A zinnia is already a zinnia as a cutting and remains one during the entire process of its growth up to blossoming, even though the flower bears its name on account of its blossom."[1]

The illustration is not incidental. The issues of human nature and destiny revealed in their fullness by the person and destiny of Jesus of Nazareth are budding issues which bloom in surprising ways. This metaphor of a zinnia that is always a zinnia but only called a zinnia on account of its blossom reflects the central theme of this chapter. "If there were only a single such flower, we could not determine its nature in advance; and yet, over the period of its growth it would still be what it revealed itself to be at the end."[2] The unique flower is, of course, Jesus—the twin bloom of Jesus and humanity.

Or to put it into more philosophical terms, Pannenberg advocates the concept of wholeness for the issues of Christology, theology and anthropology considered in this chapter.

> Only through the relation to the whole of humanity in its history, only through the eschatological import of [Jesus'] appearing and his history, can the unity of Jesus with God be expressed. This unity announces conversely (from God's perspective) that God was incarnate in this person. Through this relation to the whole of humanity in its history, the relation of each human life to the God revealed in Jesus is disclosed in the light of the history of Jesus as the new Adam.[3]

There is a great deal of thought packed into the bud of Pannenberg's flowering thought. This chapter will endeavor to capture a bit of the flower's essence in regard to Christology and anthropology.

II. "From Above" Or "From Below"?

Pannenberg employs a synthesizing approach that is both thorough and analytical. Before arriving at any conclusion he first gathers the essential elements of several related strands of thought. Analyzing each strand Pannenberg demonstrates how each is a necessary corresponding balance to another, though in the end not entirely sufficient in itself.

"Christology is concerned, therefore, not only with *unfolding* the Christian community's confession of Christ, but above all with *grounding* it in the activity and fate of Jesus in the past."[4] The "Christ of faith" and the "Jesus of history" must be considered in concert. To pursue Christology only on the basis of what Christians have confessed about the Christ will turn Christology into a discussion of the nature of faith. Even given that it is possible to analyze the historical development of Christian creeds from the primitive Church—'Ιησοῦς Κύριος, "Jesus is Lord" (I Corinthians 12:3)—through Chalcedon, the Reformation and into modern times, in the end all that can be shown is what Christians have confessed about Christ, but not the basis for such confession. "This confession itself must be grounded by Christology."[5]

Yet a biography of Jesus of Nazareth will not suffice either. For a purely historical account of Jesus is already colored by the interpretation given by the New Testament evangelists. Furthermore, given the state of affairs resulting from the work of historical criticism of the New Testament writings, a purely historical account is even more elusive. Nevertheless the purpose of history for Christology is not simply *that* Jesus lived. "Christology must go behind the New Testament to the base to which it points and which supports faith in Jesus... Christology has to ask and show the extent to which this history substantiates faith in Jesus."[6]

Herein lies the insufficiency of a Christology either entirely "from above" or entirely "from below." The former is conducive to the "Christ of faith" line of discussion. Presupposed as an object of faith, the Second Person of the Trinity, the Λόγος, assumed a human nature. "For us and for our salvation" this Λόγος ἐν σαρκός set out upon a circular path of descent to earthly human existence and death, followed by ascent in resurrection and ascension to the right hand of the Majesty on high.

Yet this approach is insufficient for it is loaded with preconceptions. "Those who speak about God being man must have some preconceptions of what is meant by the two terms."[7] A general concept of God is presupposed along with a general concept of humanity. This leads, however, not to Christology but to the nature of human faith.

Nevertheless Pannenberg also faults the "from below" line of discussion for having its own set of preconceptions. "It is exposed to the danger of using a general anthropology that is not conceived in terms of the God of the revelation in Christ as the basis of its interpretation of the coming and the special history of Jesus."[8] A Christology "from below" cannot say any more than *that* Jesus lived and died unless presuppositions are made. A general anthropology is presupposed that is potentially open to some influence "from above."[9] Pannenberg supports Otto Weber's critique: "No one can ascend from a 'below' which is something given toward an 'above' without holding this 'above' to be likewise at least potentially given in or with the 'below.'"[10]

Pannenberg does not allow these insufficiencies to rest. The conclusion is that "from above" and "from below" cannot stand as one without the other. There is a "reciprocal conditioning"[11] going on between the two. Concepts of God, even preconceptions of God, are conditioned by concepts and preconceptions about humanity, and vice versa. Still, Pannenberg does not concede to a hopeless circularity in this conclusion. "Man is truly man only in openness to God, to the future...and in loving dedication to the neighbor."[12] At the same time such a conclusion concerning the nature of man "become[s] possible only within the realm of Christendom."[13]

For Pannenberg, therefore, "above" and "below" are useful only to a point. As terms reflecting historical trends in Christological studies they are helpful. As terms to identify current systems of thought they are also helpful. But in the final analysis they are not helpful, for both must be considered at the same time. Any discussion of the general nature of humanity and the nature of the Second Person of the Trinity in order to set the stage for discussing the uniqueness of Jesus *vis à vis* humanity must be balanced by the discussion of the particularity of the work and fate of Jesus. Then it is possible to interpret from this discussion a universal significance in Jesus for humanity, together with the confession of his deity.[14] Only in this way can the uniqueness of the person and history of Jesus connect with human nature and destiny.

III. The New Man

"Jesus is at the same time the revelation of the human nature and of the destiny of man."[15] As was observed above, Pannenberg's method is to begin with Jesus and work out from there to humanity and God. The true nature of humanity is revealed in Jesus, but ultimately revealed in the destiny of humanity. The destiny of humanity, however, is revealed only through the destiny of Jesus. Thus through both Jesus' deeds and Jesus' fate humanity can learn its own nature and destiny.[16] Not only is this a *true* revelation, it is also a *new* revelation.

The contrast between Jesus as the new man and the old man of humanity is rooted deeply in Christian tradition. Paul contrasts Jesus the "second Adam" with the first Adam. The first Adam is the disobedient bringer of death to humanity. Jesus, the second Adam, through obedience, brings life.[17] Pannenberg finds in this basic contrast the point of departure for explicating the issues of human sin and salvation within the issues of human nature and destiny. Once again, however, these issues are known retrospectively in the light of the revelation of the new man in Jesus Christ, who is the fulfillment of human destiny.[18]

In this way Pannenberg faults traditional Christian doctrines which attempt to explicate fully the beginnings. Any attempt to define fully the original state of Adam, the nature of the original fall as a human being, are issues that can be discussed only retrospectively in Pannenberg's point of view. The order of questions for Pannenberg is not "What sort of man was Adam? What sort of fall did he inaugurate and, therefore, what sort of Savior does he need?" Rather in the light of Jesus' acts and fate—the full life, death and resurrection of the new man—the question becomes "What is revealed about Adam's heirs in the light of the new Adam?" "Only in the light of the revelation of the 'new man' in Jesus Christ as being the fulfillment of the specifically human destiny is it possible to know 'retrospectively' the universality of the sin seen in the figure of Adam as representative of all human beings."[19]

This same preoccupation with beginnings as applied to human beings and now in the person of Jesus is also misguided according to Pannenberg. Incarnation, the taking on of flesh by the Λόγος, cannot be isolated as a phenomenon at the birth of Jesus. "The significance of [Jesus' birth] is dependent on the story of his overall earthly course. Only in the light of what followed may we say whose birth this truly was, namely, that of the Son of God."[20]

Retrospective incarnation spread over an entire life is the way Jesus Christ is revealed as the new man and humanity itself is revealed to be what it is by the new man Jesus. "No one has a full personal identity from the moment of birth. Who we are or were, whose birth will be recalled, is seen and decided only in the course of life and in view of its end."[21]

Before one can say anything about the nature and destiny of humanity, one must wait until the end of humanity. But how is one to know the end? The end of humanity is revealed in the life of Jesus, a life also revealed fully only by his own destiny.

IV. The Author of a New Humanity

Jesus, in his person, has become the fulfillment of human destiny. Pannenberg outlines three focuses of Jesus' life and deeds which reveal not only his own destiny but also his place as humanity's representative before God, embodying human destiny in his own person. These three focuses are: Jesus' devotion to his office as the new man, Jesus' fate (his crucifixion) and Jesus' glorification by God in the resurrection.[22]

"The office of Jesus was to call men into the Kingdom of God, which had appeared with him."[23] Revealing his own Lutheran roots, Pannenberg finds significance in the term "office," *Amt*, as something given to Jesus, which makes what Jesus does truly new.[24] Nevertheless Pannenberg's acceptance of the fullness of the term does not then allow him to be drawn into the classical division of Jesus' office into its threefold nature—prophet, priest and king. The deficiency of the doctrine concerning the threefold office is that it posits Jesus as a God-man office bearer from the beginning. For Pannenberg, the conclusion that Jesus is the God-man can be made only at the culmination of his work. "Jesus appeared at the beginning not as a God-man but as a man, and as a man he knew himself to be under a mission, an office, and assignment from Israel's God."[25]

Thus for Pannenberg the traditional doctrine of the threefold office is helpful only as a symbol for relating Jesus' activity to its setting within the context of Israel's tradition of prophets, priests and kings.[26] *Amt* too must be explained by the fulfillment of Jesus' work; not the presupposition for his work.

In this discussion of Jesus' devotion to his office, the first issue of importance is the "new" aspect of the *Amt* of Jesus; a newness brought about by the imminent expectation Jesus had of the kingdom of God: "The kingdom of heaven is at hand."[27] This imminent kingdom was revealed by Jesus' resurrection from the dead. Again, retrospectively, the destiny of humanity revealed in the message of Jesus, the bearer of a *Predigtamt*, is revealed in Jesus' resurrection.

The preaching of Jesus reveals the provisional character of human life. "Man as man is always something more than and extending beyond his present situation; his destiny is not fulfilled in any given framework of his life."[28] The "something more" of humanity grows out of Jesus' own imminent expectations concerning the kingdom. Pannenberg allows for a human "openness for new possibilities," but anchored in anthropology alone there is also always the danger of "collapse" and "atrophy" of a closed present in the face of possibility.[29] Jesus' office gives the creative impulse for new possibilities.

Secondly, "the nearness of the Kingdom of God that [Jesus] proclaimed is itself salvation for those who take notice of it."[30] This too is future oriented. Where the message about the nearness of God that Jesus preached is grasped in trust, there salvation is already effective. But what is this salvation? It is not the process of being saved, but the result of being saved, that is, the full, whole fellowship of life with God. It is the future present.[31]

While Pannenberg again and again points to the future as the full revelation of many things, including salvation, still it is the nature of Jesus' *Amt* that in his preaching the accepting hearer receives that which is new in Jesus. This is shown in the writings of the evangelists in Jesus' absolving sinners without any preconditions for forgiveness, his eating with the unclean now but in the future cleansed sinners, and the healing of the sick and lame as evidence of the presence of future fulfillment.

Thirdly, Jesus' devotion to his office reveals the fatherhood of God. The nearness of the kingdom in Jesus' preaching and the presence of future salvation in the accepting hearer of the message points to God as Father. For Pannenberg, the revealing of God as Father also reveals the true nature of creation and humanity. This revelation is oriented toward the future. God is Father in relation to humanity restored proleptically to fellowship in the life and fate of Jesus. The "real significance [of the things of creation] becomes clear only when it becomes apparent what ultimately will become of them."[32] For this reason, Jesus uses the ordinary things of creation in his preaching not only to illustrate the future fulfillment present in his message, but also because the elements of his illustrations are defined by their own future destiny in God the Father.

A fourth aspect of Jesus' devotion to his office is love. Love is not a utopian ideal for Jesus, nor the fulfillment of a pre-given law. Rather, Pannenberg sees in Jesus' definition of love "the power imparted to the hearer by the message...of eschatological salvation, equipping him in turn in concrete situations to make the future possible for the neighbor in need of such assistance."[33] This fourth aspect will be developed more fully in the final portion of this chapter.

Having introduced the four aspects of Jesus' office as the Christ, these aspects can be viewed from Pannenberg's central concern: the resurrection. For Pannenberg, Jesus' devotion to his office is not a beginning point from which to proceed to other issues. For the claim that in the person of Jesus the future of God is present cannot be appreciated without discussing the resurrection.[34] Furthermore, to identify any point in the life and work of Jesus as the grounding point from which to advance conclusions is a misguided step. As noted above, the starting point is not Jesus' birth; because for Pannenberg, the incarnation is not limited to Jesus' birth but rather encompasses the whole of his life. Nor is the baptism of Jesus the starting point, nor any other event in the life of Jesus. Even the resurrection does not stand alone as a meaningful event in the life of Jesus.[35]

The resurrection of Jesus is an event of confirmation with retroactive power.[36] In the light of Easter, the message of Jesus pertaining to the imminent Kingdom of God is confirmed as well as the person of Jesus, the new man in whom the imminent Kingdom has come near. This confirmation becomes a present reality for the person who has faith in Jesus.

The concepts of imminence and prolepsis do not mean that time comes to an end in Jesus' message.

The end did not actually come before the generation of Jesus passed
away... Nevertheless for Jesus himself the final salvation of the rule
of God became a reality with his resurrection from the dead...
Through the risen Lord and his Spirit eschatological salvation had
already become a certainty for believers, so that the length of the
remaining span of time was a secondary matter.[37]

Here the reciprocal conditioning in Pannenberg's thought can be
seen clearly. He begins with a man, Jesus, whose words and deeds are
seen to be those of the new man. These implications are confirmed
only at the end with this man's resurrection. Nevertheless the end
retroactively empowers the words and deeds so that the accepting hearer
of the message preached by this man Jesus is caught up proleptically in
what will be fully revealed at the end for humanity. Not only is that
which will be revealed in the end present only in such fulfillment, but
also it is present retroactively to the hearer through this new man, Jesus.
Since the resurrection of Jesus is central to Pannenberg's thought, his
understanding of Jesus' death and his resurrection will be considered in
more depth.

V. The Death of Jesus

"Jesus death on the cross is revealed in the light of the resurrection
as the punishment suffered in our place for the blasphemous existence
of humanity."[38] Resurrection and substitution are seen in Jesus' death.
Because Pannenberg bases everything on the resurrection of Jesus, the
death of Jesus might be construed as simply an integral part of his
earthly existence as a human being. Jesus must die to be fully human,
and be raised by God in confirmation of his humanity. Clearly,
however, this is insufficient in the light of the New Testament. Death
is an essential consequence of sin rather than an arbitrary punishment
of God.[39] Far from the resurrection of Jesus depreciating the death of
Jesus, it will be seen below that, for Pannenberg, the resurrection
vindicates the need for the death of Jesus.[40]

The relationship between Jesus' fate and his previous activity
cannot be overlooked. Pannenberg sees in the Jewish accusation of
blasphemy against Jesus the central issue for Jesus' work and death.
"Had Jesus' claim to authority not proved itself to be legitimate [in the
resurrection], if one did not believe with the disciples in its future

confirmation but judged it only in the light of what was presently at hand, then Jesus could very easily appear to be a blasphemer."[41]

On the basis of present perception Jesus was guilty of blasphemy, and Jesus' death served to vindicate the Law of God and of Israel. However, with the resurrection of Jesus what was perceived as blasphemous—Jesus' carrying out of his office—is revealed to have been done by God's authority. The just law that demanded Jesus' death for the crime of blasphemy is turned now toward those who are truly blasphemous—those who acted against the authority of God by rejecting the work of Jesus.[42]

Following Paul's argument in Romans, Pannenberg interprets the Jewish law concerning blasphemy to contain an universal application for humanity's relation to God. Sin and death are not merely Jewish phenomena; they are universal. "Man is subjected to death just because of his being closed in on himself, while his destiny to openness to the world still points beyond death."[43]

The destiny of humanity is revealed in Jesus' resurrection. In contrast humanity looks for meaning for the existing world within the world itself, or in humanity's present earthly life. So as Paul claims, and Pannenberg supports, the death of Jesus as the means to human destiny has been rejected by both Jew and Gentile alike, universal humanity. By choosing to find meaning in the present rather than in the future destiny of humanity, all of humanity becomes blasphemous.[44]

The cross of Jesus is not only an accusation of blasphemy against a rejecting humanity. It is also the vindication of Jesus through his resurrection. The instrument of accusation toward humanity is also an instrument of salvation for humanity. This relationship between accusation and salvation leads Pannenberg to question traditional themes of atonement in Christian doctrine. He rejects the ransom theory of atonement because any real understanding of ransom "concedes to the devil a right to power over humanity."[45]

The satisfaction theories, as pioneered by Anselm of Canterbury, rest upon the understanding of Jesus' death as something which Jesus himself has accomplished. Pannenberg counters that even though the Gospels portray Jesus' determination to go to his death and his predictions of the same, still his death was something that happened to him. Jesus is obedient unto death, as Paul writes in Philippians, yet ultimately it is God who is acting through Jesus in giving him up as a sacrifice.[46]

Once again Pannenberg follows in the tradition of Martin Luther.

Jesus' suffering is a suffering *pro nobis*, for us, a vicarious suffering. The cross, which in the light of the resurrection has become an accusation of blasphemy against humanity, is the means by which Jesus in fact carries the charge for which he was crucified—blasphemy. "Luther thus recognized the meaning of Jesus' death in the fact that the punishment for our sin [of blasphemy] happened to him."[47]

Pannenberg parts company with the Reformer over the basis for the penal suffering of Jesus as the Christ for us. For Luther the cross was the *terminus ad quem* of the incarnation. Incarnation, for Luther, was limited to the birth of Jesus as the *terminus ab quo*. Thus Luther held that God became man in order to suffer and die for humanity, that humanity might be raised to God—Luther's "joyous exchange."[48] Pannenberg, on the other hand, holds that the incarnation applies to the whole life of Jesus, finding its significance not from the beginning, but from Jesus' destiny. "Luther did not clearly see that all statements about Jesus' cross are only possible in the light of his resurrection."[49]

Always keeping Easter in view Pannenberg holds that Jesus' death befell him from the hands of humanity due to his perceived blasphemous authority to say and do what he did. The resurrection, however, vindicated all that Jesus said and did. Thus the charge brought against Jesus becomes the indictment of humanity which has blasphemously executed a vindicated man. The death on the cross then is the event by which God vicariously answers humanity's guilt of blasphemy against Jesus through the means of Jesus' own vindication in the resurrection.

Pannenberg's understanding of Jesus' relationship to humanity needs further explication. "Representation and expiation [the place of Jesus and his fate on the cross] do not mean that those represented do not have to die themselves. [There is no substitution, no satisfaction for humanity in Jesus' death.] It means, rather, that those whom Jesus represents have the possibility in their death, by reason of its linking to the death of Jesus, of attaining to the hope of participating in the new resurrection life that has already become manifest in Jesus."[50] Because of the resurrection of Jesus from death, humanity in fellowship with Jesus is given the hope that its own death is not finally a separation from life with God. Because Jesus shared humanity's death, humanity may share Jesus' resurrection.

VI. The Resurrection of Jesus

The resurrection of Jesus from the dead is the all encompassing theme of Pannenberg's Christology. The resurrection has been the horizon for all that has been discussed, and therefore it has an important place in Pannenberg's Christologically derived anthropology. "The resurrection of Jesus is the basis of the Christian faith, yet not as an isolated event, but in its reference back to the earthly sending of Jesus and his death on the cross."[51]

The younger Pannenberg in his book, *Jesus—God and Man*, begins with the proleptic element in Jesus' resurrection. As has been noted repeatedly, all that Jesus did is vindicated in the resurrection, but the same resurrection is present retroactively/proleptically in what Jesus did and said before that event.

The term "retroactive" has already been introduced above. It is a term, borrowed from law, that is used by Pannenberg with some frequency in *Jesus—God and Man*.[52] In that book Pannenberg outlines the resurrection as a retroactive power, *rückwirkende Kraft*. As *Kraft*, power, there is an active element understood as affecting both Jesus' life and human life in retrospect, *rückwirkung*, before resurrection. Nevertheless, the retroactive nature of this power is such that until the fulfillment in the resurrection there can be no comprehension of the full effects of the power upon Jesus' life or humanity's life. The confirmation of the resurrection reveals what was hidden in Jesus' pre-Easter work, even though the power of the resurrection was at work retroactively. Pannenberg confesses that this *rückwirkende Kraft* is foreign to ontological thought, yet it holds a unique relevance in the case of Jesus.[53] In the mature thought of his *Systematic Theology*, Pannenberg uses the term "metaphor" to color this retroactive element. Because the resurrection is something which "falls outside the realm of everyday experience [it] must be stated metaphorically."[54]

The connection between the two issues of metaphor and prolepsis is in their difference. Metaphors used for Jesus' resurrection are "sleep," "raised up/rise up," and "awake." (Pannenberg sees no contradiction between the transitive "to raise" and the intransitive "to rise." "The one who is raised up rises up."[55] Always the resurrection is held to be an act of the Father, not of the Son himself.) These metaphors are used, however, to refer to a real event—a death, a life, a raising up from death to life. The proleptic element in Jesus' resurrection is the already present authority to grant this new life through his pre-Easter office; an office yet to be vindicated by the event of Easter. Metaphor is the language used to speak of that which is so new as to be beyond the ordinary words. Prolepsis is the already present reality—already present because of the retroactive power of the resurrection—in the ordinary of which the metaphor speaks. "Everything depends upon the connection between Jesus' claim and its confirmation by God."[56] But because vindication, universal human significance, death and life are all bound up in the resurrection, Pannenberg calls the language metaphorical. It is not mythical language implying a reality beyond experience, but a metaphorical language referring to real events. It is because the real events are proleptic, not fully realized in everyday experience but only in the future, that the events must be stated metaphorically.[57]

These events are defined by six significant points which Pannenberg deduces from Jesus' resurrection:

1. If Jesus has been raised, the end of the world has begun.
2. If Jesus has been raised, this for a Jew can only mean that God himself has confirmed the pre-Easter activity of Jesus.
3. Through [the] resurrection...the Son of Man is none other than the man Jesus who will come again.
4. If Jesus, having been raised from the dead, is ascended to God and if already the end of the world has begun, then God is ultimately revealed in Jesus.
5. The transition to the Gentile mission is motivated by the eschatological resurrection of Jesus.
6. The words of the risen Jesus [according to Christian tradition, are] the explication of the significance inherent in the resurrection itself.[58]

These significant points will be traced through this chapter on Jesus' resurrection as well as in the final portion dealing with anthropology.

Given these six points, Pannenberg seeks to demonstrate the present possibility and reality of that which is described metaphorically. He does this by tracing the Jewish eschatological roots (number 2 and 5 above) of the Christian message concerning Jesus' resurrection.

Tracing the emergence of resurrection thought from the period of the Babylonian exile, the Jewish understanding of resurrection emerged from the conflict between the justice of God and the display of that justice in the lives of individuals. Observation concerning the course of the world and human events revealed that the righteous do suffer and the wicked prosper—contrary to the accepted wisdom of a righteous life rewarded and wickedness punished.

To balance the justice of God with such a state of affairs in the course of human events the idea of a future reward or punishment for good or bad deeds was worked out. "But this thought demanded a resurrection of the dead such as we find expressly in the OT only in Daniel 12:2."[59] This general resurrection for the purpose of reward or judgement was modified over time to focus only on a resurrection of the righteous to receive their reward.

So it was that by the time of Jesus' resurrection appearances to the disciples and Paul there was already an expectation that the righteous would be raised to the reward of their righteousness. "We must recognize that prior to Paul there already was a tradition in which the expectation of the resurrection of the dead was cultivated and within which Paul himself stood."[60]

This expectation stemming from the post-exilic era is what makes it possible for the disciples to recognize Jesus as being raised—neither considering him a ghost nor a resuscitated corpse returned to the same former life. The wounds of Jesus still visible according to the Gospel accounts tie the resurrection to the pre-Easter events. The experience of seeing the resurrected Jesus was prepared for in the sharing of his life with the disciples, and in the work that culminated in Jerusalem at the cross.[61] Thus the expectation of the resurrected righteous is vindicated in Jesus' resurrection at the same time that vindicated righteousness is proleptically present in the righteous work of Jesus' office.

Having surveyed the Old Testament background to the meaning of Jesus' resurrection, Pannenberg returns to the reciprocal nature of vindication. "The result is that for its final vindication, the Christian message of the resurrection of Jesus needs the events of an eschatological resurrection of the dead. The enacting of this event is one of the conditions, if not the only condition, on which to maintain the truth of the resurrection of Jesus."[62] The resurrection of Jesus vindicates the expectation for the life of the righteous, but it will be the resurrection of all the righteous that will vindicate the reality of Jesus' resurrection (and the proleptic presence of Jesus' resurrection at work in the life of the righteous!).

Finally, Pannenberg takes up the issue of the historicity of Jesus' resurrection along with the eschatological vindication that Jesus' resurrection has indeed taken place. The historicity of the resurrection has concerned Pannenberg throughout his career. At issue here are two traditions. The first is the tradition of the appearances to the disciples, and, related to this, the nature of those appearances. The second is the tradition of the empty tomb.

In order to answer the question whether Jesus did rise from the dead, Pannenberg points exclusively to Paul's words in I Corinthians 15:1-11. He considers the evangelists' accounts too tainted with mythical/legendary material. In I Corinthains 15 the apostle lists the appearances of Jesus as providing historical proof of the resurrection. This passage is sufficient, in Pannenberg's estimation, to ground historically that the disciples saw the resurrected Jesus. This passage's implied certainty derives from the time in which the epistle is written and Paul's use of already accepted phrases to describe those appearances. "In view of the age of the formulated tradition used by Paul and of the proximity of Paul to the events, the assumption that appearances of the resurrected Lord were really experienced has good historical foundation."[63]

That a resurrected Jesus was seen is sufficiently verifiable. *What* it was requires a more challenging explanation. First, the appearances may have involved a vision not visible to all. This was the case of Paul on the Damascus road. Preliminarily, Pannenberg concludes that "'visions' can only express something of the subjective mode of experience, not something about the reality of the event experienced in this form."[64] Yet over against this conclusion Pannenberg also holds that "the Easter appearances are not to be explained from the Easter faith of the disciples; rather, conversely, the Easter faith of the disciples is to be explained from the appearances."[65]

So vision becomes a metaphor for what the disciples experienced. A limiting of the term "vision" as only a term reflecting the subjective nature of the one having the vision gets amended to include an understanding of vision as something embodying a reality in the vision. Again in reciprocal fashion, the openness of the eschatologically expectant disciples to the resurrection of the righteous does not induce the vision of a resurrected Lord. Rather the vision of a truly resurrected Jesus vindicates that expectation.

Complicating the historicity argument is the claim that what has happened in Jesus' resurrection is new. Here, Pannenberg resorts to metaphor. "The resurrected Lord is in fact not perceptible as one object among others in the world; therefore, he could only be experienced and designated by an extraordinary mode of experience, the vision, and only in metaphorical language."[66]   Is Pannenberg defeating his own argument by retreating into faith? No, but neither is he trying to argue a skeptic into faith via history.   Rather, Pannenberg is laying out the reasonable probability that what the New Testament writers have written did take place apart from their own subjectivity.

The empty tomb tradition bolsters the high probability of an historical resurrection of Jesus.   While granting that the finding of an empty tomb is no proof in itself that Jesus was raised and that the effect of the empty tomb would be of interest only to the inhabitants of Jerusalem and vicinity, still this tradition stands along side the appearances as support for the historical resurrection.[67]

Pannenberg argues that for the early Church it was the appearances of the resurrected Jesus that were important—even though the Gospel of Mark emphasizes the empty tomb.   However, precisely because the disciples and Paul have no connection with the tomb and Jesus' burial, the presence of the empty tomb tradition nonetheless is compelling. "By their mutually complementing each other [the appearance tradition and the grave tradition] let the assertion of the reality of Jesus' resurrection...appear as historically very probable, and that always means in historical inquiry that it is to be presupposed until contrary evidence appears."[68]

Pannenberg's argument regarding the historicity of the resurrection lays the foundation for discussing its significance for all of humanity. The proleptic/retroactive understanding of the resurrection of Jesus both for his own person and work governs an understanding of human destiny proleptically revealed by the resurrected Jesus.   The precise connection between the resurrected Jesus and human destiny will be treated below in the section on anthropology.   In order to gain a clearer sense of Pannenberg's Christology, and thus its importance for anthropology, some critical observations will be surveyed.

VII. Critics

This brief survey of criticism of Pannenberg's understanding of the resurrection will reveal how challenging his approach is for some to accept. More importantly, the items of critique demonstrate precisely at which points Pannenberg's thought can lead to possible misinterpretations.

One supportive critic is David McKenzie. In a brief analysis of Pannenberg's argument concerning the resurrection, McKenzie divides the argument into two parts—historical and philosophical. McKenzie does not criticize the historical argument in favor of the historicity of the resurrection based on the two traditions of appearances and the empty tomb. It is the philosophical argument that he considers deficient. McKenzie deems Pannenberg's philosophical argument successful in that Pannenberg does show convincingly a bias among humanity against belief in the resurrection. But demonstrating "bias against" is not the same as a convincing argument for acceptance. "[The philosophical argument] does not function well as an argument for the existence of God."[69]

What McKenzie overlooks is that while the resurrection argument is pivotal, it does not stand alone. The historical and philosophical arguments turn the skeptic/unbeliever toward entertaining the possibility of resurrection. This turning toward possibility is already a turning from the destructiveness of a humanity turned in upon itself (*curvatus in se*). This entertaining of a possibility is not identical to faith, but it is potentially faith. In the light of the retroactive nature of human destiny, potential is much more than an empty possibility. An argument, even a resurrection argument, is not an "one point presented, accepted or rejected" event. It is part of the whole revealed only at the end. The philosophical incompleteness that McKenzie criticizes stems from an isolating of only one part of Pannenberg's argument.

This isolation of one aspect of his argument is exhibited by several critics of Pannenberg. In a survey of the criticism section,[70] Stanley Grenz, a student of Pannenberg's, lists critics who accuse Pannenberg's retroactivity of adoptionism—once again seeing the resurrection as a single point rather than Pannenberg's insistence that the resurrection is something which encompasses the whole life and destiny of Jesus and humanity.[71] While it may be an oversimplification of his critics, many of the criticisms concerning the different aspects of Pannenberg's thought isolate one aspect from the whole, which when once isolated is not capable of standing on its own without the whole argument.

Pannenberg's use of metaphor is also strongly criticized. On the one hand critics accuse him of denying a literal bodily resurrection by using the evasive term of metaphor. Yet, Pannenberg uses metaphor to emphasize the reality of Jesus' resurrection while at the same time it avoids any suggestion that the resurrection is a resuscitation of a corpse back to its former life. There are critics who accuse Pannenberg of moving into myth by using the term metaphor.[72] Reginald Fuller, however, applauds Pannenberg's move. "It is wholly in keeping with the nature of the event."[73] Fuller understands that for Pannenberg to demonstrate just how "new" this new man, Jesus, truly is, metaphor is the only language available to the "old" humanity to describe the new.

A third area of criticism of Pannenberg's argument is directed toward his move from the particular in Jesus to the universal in humanity. This issue will be considered more fully in the following section. If there is a significant newness in Jesus—his atoning death and vindicating resurrection—does this newness separate him from universal humanity? Conversely, given this newness, what is there in humanity that can serve in the vindication of Jesus' newness? Pannenberg, for his part, is confident and persists.

> The hermeneutical concern for a dependence of each and all particular meanings on the framework of a totality of meaning is related to the field concept [of organic unity in evolutionary biology]...I am, of course, aware of the audacity of the attempt at such a conceptual integration. But then, such is inevitable when a theologian even begins to realize what is required in talking about God.[74]

VIII. Anthropology

Pannenberg's anthropology is characterized by the same scope and depth as his Christology. For Pannenberg:

> A full anthropology would have to include...the actualizing of [human] destiny, which is the theme of God's redeeming work, its appropriation to and by us, and its goal in the eschatological consummation. A full anthropology would also include not only the biological foundations of the human form of life, its nature, and its position in the world but also the social relations in which human life is lived.[75]

Therefore, in the light of what a "full anthropology" would include, this section of the chapter will limit the discussion of anthropological issues to those which correspond to issues raised in the Christological section.

This section will continue to employ the method of reciprocal conditioning, which is a consequence of Pannenberg's concept of the whole. Christology impacts anthropology and anthropology Christology. The destiny of humanity is fellowship with God.[76] But understanding this fellowship with God is developed on the basis of the creation of humanity in the image of God. Thus, while some of the fullness of Pannenberg's anthropology will appear in this section, the emphasis will be on the issue of our human destiny and, conversely, the situations of our alienation from that destiny.

Central to Pannenberg's anthropology is the concept of the image of God. Pannenberg approaches the question of the image of God not as an original state of humanity; a state that has subsequently become lost. Rather, he insists on an approach that begins with what is ordinarily seen in the present condition of the image of God in humanity.[77]

Pannenberg begins to discuss the concept of the image of God by appealing to the 18th century philosopher, J. G. von Herder.[78] Herder understood the image of God as a directive force, an understanding that lends itself to Pannenberg's own understanding of humanity moving towards its destiny. For Herder, the image of God is, first of all, the guide for human beings (as instinct is the guide for animals). Secondly, this guiding image of God serves for the achieving of an end. "We are not yet men, but are daily *becoming* so."[79] Thirdly, human beings cannot become human by themselves, but, finally, the guiding image of God uses tradition and learning, reason and experience and divine providence to achieve the destiny toward which it guides humanity.[80] The image of God is an already present guide in humanity, but it is a teleologically oriented, already-present guide, being revealed fully only upon achieving the destiny of humanity.

Pannenberg relates this general nexus between humanity and God through this "image" to the treatment of the "image of God" in the New Testament. The Pauline statements concerning the image of God are applied almost exclusively to Jesus.[81] These verses, while they speak of Jesus and not universal humanity, nonetheless provide the basis for a uniting of God and humanity in the particular *imago Dei* of Jesus. This unity provides Pannenberg with the destiny-oriented focus that he subsequently explicates.

It is in the light of human destiny that one can see both those attributes of humanity that serve to achieve that destiny, and those attributes which militate against human destiny. Ironically, the same elements of humanity can be both destructive and productive of the destiny of fellowship with God. This dual potential of human attributes is Pannenberg's way of avoiding the conclusion that the human creation itself is inherently evil. This duality is the case because we human beings live and lead our lives consciously.[82]

One such attribute is the human ego. The human ego, that personal self which is the embodiment of the guiding image of God, acts in relation to the other. "The being with others as others mediated by perception awareness thus seems to include, along with the distinction of objects from one another and from the I of one's own body, a field of consciousness in which the basic relation of I and the world takes on its contours."[83]

It is this "ego conscious of the other" that serves the destiny of humanity. The present world, the past and the future, are "others" that teach the ego. God, Jesus, other human beings are "others" which, through experience, instruct the ego. The ego, conscious of itself and the other, is conscious of itself set in relation to the other. When the ego is set in relation against the other, or when the presence of the other becomes the opportunity for the ego to dominate or turn from the other—whether the "other" is human, the world or God—destiny is impinged. This leads to Pannenberg's understanding of alienation/sin.

For Pannenberg, alienation is an ancient Christian term and not simply borrowed from modern psychology.[84] Since the being of humanity is bound up with the future to which we are destined—fellowship with God—alienation is a "being closed off to God," and therefore closed off to the future that is humanity's destiny.[85] Because we are conscious beings, we are aware that this alienation can be both an action on our part as well as a situation in which we find ourselves.

Alienation as an act of humanity is traced to the condition of humanity being turned in on itself (*curvatus in se*). A human ego that is conscious of the other, and yet turns away from the other to self due to fear, pride, etc, becomes alienated. A conscious ego turning away from the human destiny of fellowship with God is an alienating act which Christian tradition has called sin. For Pannenberg, the definition of sin is derived from destiny, defining sin in terms of alienation from that destiny of humanity.

Working from destiny back retrospectively to Adam, it was Adam's turning away from fellowship with God that was his undoing. To find his destiny in an other besides God led to alienation. Jesus, the second Adam, is obedient to the guiding of human destiny. His obedient ego is revealed by his achieving his destiny in the resurrection.

Anthropologically speaking, human misery and death then "is the lot of those who are deprived of the fellowship with God that is the destiny of human life."[86] Pannenberg prefers the term "misery" to the term "sin." "The term 'misery' sums up our detachment from God, our autonomy, and all the resultant consequences."[87] Alienated from God—proleptically and/or ultimately—humanity lives in the misery of separation from God.

In this way Pannenberg considers death as the ultimate consequence of alienation. For if destiny is life with God, what is our separation from this destiny but death? Death is for Pannenberg a consequence of sin, not an arbitrary punishment by God. Furthermore, since Pannenberg views death as a consequence of alienation, it cannot fulfill human destiny. "The only question, then, is whether in death there is an opening to God as there was in the death of Jesus, or whether on the contrary there is a closing of the self to God, so that death is under the sign of sin."[88]

Pannenberg criticizes Rahner as one who advocates a human fulfillment of life in death. Pannenberg calls this "dubious."[89] "Death does not bring life to its fulfillment but terminates it and prevents its fulfillment."[90] It is here that we arrive at the nexus of Jesus' destiny in his death, and humanity's being cut short of destiny by death.

Stepping back once again to the issue of alienation, Pannenberg notes that not all acts of alienation are the acts of a human ego against its destiny. Alienation may come from situations of the other that militate against a destiny-focused self.[91] For human beings live in relation to other human beings in society. The human being lives in relation to the other of the world of things. The human being lives in relation to the other of history. These are all arenas in which Pannenberg develops his anthropology.[92] In each of these arenas the human attributes of consciousness, language, freedom, openness to the future, as well as alienation and death, come into play. In all of these arenas there is a tension that remains between the "centrality" of the conscious ego and the "exocentricity" of the other-focused ego. This is the tension between the appropriate consciousness of self ("centrality") balanced with the appropriate consciousness of others ("exocentricity").

There is also the tension between human destiny to be the image of God and that egocentricity that marks the observable living of human lives terminated in death—the tension between the proleptic and the present.[93]

In all of these tension-created situations of alienation comes the misery unto death. "O wretched man that I am, who will rescue me..." (Romans 7:24) Here are the third and fourth points presented by Herder and appropriated by Pannenberg. "Human beings cannot become human by themselves." Human beings are "educated" toward their destiny by tradition and living, reason and experience as these are brought together by divine providence, i.e., the new man, Jesus. Here we arrive at the issue of Jesus' vicarious death and resurrection destiny. It is the person and work of Jesus the Christ which turns humanity from its alienated misery unto death.

While Pannenberg has advocated that for humanity to reach its destiny the new man Jesus must open what human alienation has closed, he does not employ substitutionary Christological concepts. Jesus is not the absolutely representative new man who stands in the place of alienated humanity. "It has been validly argued that a true representative only temporarily takes the place of others and thus leaves open the place that is only representatively occupied."[94] Pannenberg cautions that such representativeness can easily become exclusively substitutionary.[95]

The representation that Pannenberg advocates is that in Jesus' death, human beings

> no longer have to see themselves as excluded from fellowship with God and therefore as enemies of God. [Alienation leading to death creates this state of affairs.] [Jesus] opens up access for them so that in accepting their finitude like him, and in fellowship with him, they come to share in life from God and can already live the earthly life assured of the eternal fellowship with God that overcomes the limitation of death.[96]

Because Jesus accepted the fate laid upon him by blasphemous humanity, and yet was given vindication by God through the resurrection to life, so blasphemous/alienated humanity may, with the vindicated Son, come to the same life.

This already-present fellowship with God is what creates true openness to the future. "It also sets [human beings] at a distance from themselves which enables them to fulfill their individual callings in service to God and to the world, to which his love is addressed."[97] Here are the twin aspects of the Fatherhood of God and love which came to light for humanity in the resurrection of Jesus. It is in this "distanced selfhood" created by fellowship with Jesus in the proleptic fellowship with God that enables human beings to live out their humanity as truly human.

Pannenberg contends that this "distanced selfhood" is essential for human relatedness to the other within social situations. Issues of property, work and economy require a destiny-focused "distanced self" to be truly human issues. The same can be said for issues of sexuality, marriage and family, as well as the issues of the civil realm—politics, law and justice.[98]

A Christological view of humanity, as Pannenberg has developed it, is at once a humanity independent and dependent. In human history as it runs between the first Adam to the new Adam, there is present an independent, open to the future characteristic of human beings. Yet this independent characteristic is not the essential nature of humanity. Humanity's essential nature has been defined by Jesus' destiny, making humanity also destiny-focused beings.[99]

Like marriage mentioned above, human beings of different sexes are individuals, but not individuals alone. There is a fellowship of unity in marriage. So also the new destiny brought to light by the resurrection of Jesus Christ is not for him alone. It is a destiny proleptically present in human history with a retroactive power creating a community of new humanity with Jesus in anticipation of the final confirmation in the eschaton.

Pannenberg himself can best summarize his understanding of anthropology in the light of Christology as a conclusion to this chapter:

> As one eschatological summation, as the reconciliation of humanity across all dividing chasms, the Christ event establishes not only the unity of human history, but thereby also establishes the unity of the universe. This assertion presupposes that the totality of the material world does not possess its unity in itself apart from man, but that this unity is only structured through man. The cosmos is not in itself a unity...which is given prior to man and merely copied in him as the microcosmos. Rather, the multiplicity of things in nature is first united to form the world through men...Precisely when [man] creates the world out of things he finds, man is God's image, God's viceroy

in the world...In this sense, the history of Jesus, on the basis of which humanity is embraced into the unity of a single history, is at the same time the consummation of the unity of the world. As humanity in its history, so too the material universe is only brought together to the unity of a world through its relation to Jesus.[100]

Notes

1. Wolfhart Pannenberg, *Metaphysics and the Idea of God* (Grand Rapids: Wm. B. Eerdmans Publishing Co., 1990), 105.

2. Ibid.

3. Ibid., 146.

4. Wolfhart Pannenberg, *Jesus—God and Man* (Philadelphia: Westminster Press, 1977), 28.

5. Ibid., 29.

6. Ibid.

7. Wolfhart Pannenberg, *Systematic Theology, Volume 2* (Grand Rapids: Wm. B. Eerdmans Publishing Co., 1994), 290.

8. Ibid.

9. Pannenberg, *Jesus—God and Man*, 35.

10. Ibid. Weber's contention is that the presupposition for thinking "from below" is the openness of that "below" to the divine "above." Cf. Otto Weber, *Grundlagen der Dogmatik, Volume II*, p.26ff.

11. Pannenberg, *Systematic Theology, Vol. 2*, 290.

12. Pannenberg, *Jesus—God and Man*, 202-203.

13. Ibid.

14. Pannenberg, *Systematic Theology, Vol. 2*, 296.

15. Pannenberg, *Jesus—God and Man*, 191.

16. Ibid., 193.

17. Cf. Romans 5:12-21.

18. Wolfhart Pannenberg, *Anthropology in Theological Perspective* (Philadelphia: Westminster Press, 1985), 136.

19. Ibid.

20. Pannenberg, *Systematic Theology, Vol. 2*, 302.

21. Ibid.

22. Pannenberg, *Jesus—God and Man*, 195.

23. Ibid., 212.

24. Ibid.

25. Ibid., 223.

26. Ibid., 235.

27. Cf. Matthew 4:14, Mark 1:15.

28. Pannenberg, *Jesus—God and Man*, 226.

29. Ibid., 227.

30. Ibid.

31. Pannenberg, *Systematic Theology, Vol. 2*, 399.

32. Pannenberg, *Jesus—God and Man*, 230.

33. Ibid.

34. Pannenberg, *Systematic Theology, Vol. 2*, 365.

35. Pannenberg, *Systematic Theology, Vol. 2*, 365.

36. Ibid. The concept of "retroactive power" (*rückwirkende Kraft*) is significant in Pannenberg's *Jesus—God and Man*, 135ff. This concept will be discussed more fully in section *VI. The Resurrection of Jesus*.

37. Pannenberg, *Systematic Theology, Vol. 2*, 366.

38. Pannenberg, *Jesus—God and Man*, 245.

39. Pannenberg, *Systematic Theology, Vol. 2*, 338.

40. Ibid.

41. Pannenberg, *Jesus—God and Man*, 253.

42. Ibid., 255.

43. Ibid., 262.

44. Ibid.

45. Ibid., 276.

46. Ibid., 277.

47. Ibid., 278.

48. Cf. page 44, note 62, on Luther, "The Freedom of a Christian."

49. Pannenberg, *Jesus—God and Man*, 279.

50. Pannenberg, *Systematic Theology, Vol. 2*, 427.

51. Ibid., 344.

52. Pannenberg, *Jesus—God and Man*, 135; cf. Wolfhart Pannenberg, *Grundzüge der Christologie* (Gütersloh: Gütersloh Verlagshaus Gerd Mohn, 1964), 134.

53. Pannenberg, *Jesus—God and Man*, 135. Cf. Pannenberg, *Systematic Theology, Vol. 2*, 303; also Wolfhart Pannenberg, *Systematische Theologie, Band 1* (Göttingen: Vandenhoeck & Ruprecht, 1988), 342-343.

54. Pannenberg, *Systematic Theology, Vol. 2*, 347.

55. Ibid., 376.

56. Pannenberg, *Jesus—God and Man*, 66.

57. Pannenberg, *Systematic Theology, Vol. 2*, 346.

58. Pannenberg, *Jesus—God and Man*, 67-73.

59. Pannenberg, *Systematic Theology, Vol. 2*, 347.

60. Pannenberg, *Jesus—God and Man*, 78.

61. Pannenberg, *Systematic Theology, Vol. 2*, 349.

62. Ibid., 350-351.

63. Pannenberg, *Jesus—God and Man*, 91.

64. Ibid., 95.

65. Ibid., 96.

66. Ibid., 99.

67. Ibid., 105-106.

68. Ibid., 105.

69. David McKenzie, *Wolfhart Pannenberg & Religious Philosophy* (Washington, D.C.: University Press of America, Inc., 1980), 102.

70. Carl E. Braaten & Philip Clayton, editors, *The Theology of Wolfhart Pannenberg* (Minneapolis: Augsburg Publishing House, 1988), 19-52.

71. Ibid., 41.

72. Braaten & Clayton, *The Theology of Wolfhart Pannenberg*, 39.

73. Ibid.

74. Ibid., 324.

75. Pannenberg, *Systematic Theology, Vol. 2*, 180-181.

76. Ibid., 200ff.

77. Pannenberg, *Anthropology in Theological Perspective*, 47ff.

78. Johann Gottfried von Herder (1744-1803) was a German philosopher of history. He held that the meaning of world history consists in the development of humanity, which is both the essence of all human rational tendencies and, at the same time, an ethical ideal. In his *Auch eine Philosophie der Geschichte zur Bildung der Menschheit* (1774) Herder studies history as God's action in nature and upon nations. Pannenberg cites Herder's conclusions frequently in his *Anthropology in Theological Perspective*.

79. Pannenberg, *Anthropology*, 45.

80. Ibid., 45-46.

81. Cf. II Corinthians 4:4, Colossians 1:15, Hebrews 1:3.

82. Pannenberg, *Systematic Theology, Vol. 2*, 181.

83. Ibid., 193.

84. Pannenberg, *Anthropology*, 267-269. Pannenberg cites Aristotle's use of the term to mean "a disposal of property." In the Old Testament (*LXX*) and in the New Testament there is *apellotriōmenoi*, "estranged" from God. (Psalm 58:3, Ephesians 4:18) Pannenberg also identifies the use of "alienation" among the mystics, especially Meister Eckhart.

85. Ibid., 273.

86. Pannenberg, *Systematic Theology, Vol. 2*, 178.

87. Ibid., 179.

88. Pannenberg, *Anthropology*, 139.

89. Ibid.

90. Ibid.

91. Pannenberg, *Systematic Theology, Vol. 2*, 179.

92. Pannenberg, *Anthropology*, "Part Three," 315-532.

93. Ibid., 164.

94. Pannenberg, *Systematic Theology, Vol. 2*, 432.

95. Ibid.

96. Ibid., 434.

97. Ibid., 436.

98. Pannenberg, *Anthropology*, Chapter 8, 397-484.

99. Ibid., 499-500.

100. Pannenberg, *Jesus—God and Man*, 390.

Chapter 4

Conclusions

I. Introduction

In this concluding chapter comparisons will be made between Macquarrie and Pannenberg on anthropology and Christology. The material presented in chapters two and three invite comparison because of a number of issues discussed by both. These issues of common interest will be compared below. Following these comparisons a final portion of this chapter will analyze the nature of the comparisons. Is a synthesis possible or do Macquarrie and Pannenberg present paradoxical views? Before the comparisons can be made, an overview of the methodologies of Macquarrie and Pannenberg is necessary.

II. A Summary Overview

Macquarrie

John Macquarrie uses a question posed by Dietrich Bonhoeffer as the foil for his anthropology and Christology. "Who really is Jesus Christ for us today?"[1] With this question Macquarrie begins at the end and works toward the beginning. "Us today" is the subject which yields the clearest possibility for explication.

As the second chapter explained above, Macquarrie answers Bonhoeffer's question by undertaking a "search for humanity," a discussion of who and what is a human being. Having stated the search for humanity as the quest upon which Macquarrie sets out to answer Bonhoeffer's question, he immediately also must ask, "Where does one begin?"[2] To these questions Macquarrie provides his own answers. "There is no quick inclusive answer, and we shall have to consider a great many aspects, one after the other.[3]

As Macquarrie proceeds, the attributes of human beings are considered, "one after the other." In the course of this consideration it became clear that human beings are not simply a sum of their attributes.

Macquarrie's order of attributes is not haphazard. There is a progression from the attribute of freedom, which Macquarrie calls the first and most obvious attribute,[4] through each attribute discussed. One leads to another as an elaboration, or as a related attribute to the former, in Macquarrie's progression.

The progression, however, is not simply a chain of attributes strung out linearly. As chapter two showed, there are groupings of the attributes—formative, interactive, austere, etc—which unify the human being as a being. Nevertheless, in this unified, multifaceted being called a human being, Macquarrie has demonstrated a human "becoming."

> Perhaps one should speak not of a 'human being' but of a 'human becoming,' awkward though the usage would be. We could say that we are all *becoming* human, in the sense that we are discovering and, it may be hoped, realizing what the potentials of human existence are.[5]

Thus, for Macquarrie, a human being is not only a progression of attributes collected in unifying identity as human, but also a progression (for *becoming* implies the desire to become more fully human, not less so) toward realized potentials. It is this progression of realizing potentials that leads Macquarrie to conclude that human being/becoming, more than anything else, reveals something of the creative forces at work in the universe.

> On the basis of this affinity between the life of humanity and the wider reality within which that life is set, it is possible to construct what might be called an anthropological argument for the existence of God.[6]

This anthropological argument for the existence of God leads Macquarrie to Christology. If the discussion of anthropology has presented the possibility that human beings are "beings in transcendence," becoming more fully human but at the same time growing in the capacity for Being/God, then this anthropological argument for the existence of God will lead to the realization of the God-ward possibility in Jesus Christ. As chapter two concluded above, Macquarrie's Christology is an explication of the actuality in Jesus of the potentiality in human becoming.[7] Christology results from careful anthropology.

Bonhoeffer's question, "Who really is Jesus Christ for us today?" is answered by considering who human beings are today, and potentially may be in their transcending. Jesus Christ is human possibility realized in historical actuality.[8] Thus Macquarrie's Christology is an anthropological Christology.

Pannenberg

Wolfhart Pannenberg's method challenges description because where Macquarrie begins with parts/attributes and discovers in the process a unified wholeness, Pannenberg insists on beginning with the unified whole. "The concept of the whole as the all-inclusive whole of all finite reality...becomes an explicit theme for theology whether one wishes it or not."[9] The challenge comes, as chapter three stated several times, in considering parts of anthropology and Christology but always considering the parts in the light of the whole. For without the whole the parts cannot be considered fully or accurately.

For this reason Pannenberg begins with Christology. The whole of finite reality is not absolute in itself. There is a "unifying unity" involved.[10] This unifying unity, by which Pannenberg means God, must be distinct from the whole of finite reality to be the unifying unity. Yet if distinct only, then God becomes a finite part to be considered in the whole (but no longer God). Thus God, the unifying unity, must also be immanent to the finite as the unifying unity.

Pannenberg hesitates to call this unifying unity a proof of God's existence in any formal sense, but he does consider it sufficient to support Christology as the starting point for considering the unified unity.

> Only through the relation to the whole of humanity in its history, only through the eschatological import of his appearing and his history, can the unity of Jesus with God be expressed. This unity announces conversely (from God's perspective) that God was incarnate in this person. Through this relation to the whole of humanity in its history, the relation of each human life to the God revealed in Jesus is disclosed in the light of the history of Jesus as the new Adam.[11]

Thus the person of Jesus becomes expressive of the whole of human history in his own history. Jesus is the expression of the whole with the distinct and immanent unifying unity, called God. Within this highly abstract concept of the whole, the study of humanity as individuals in contrast to the whole is possible without prejudicing the outcome. For the considerations of humanity, even individual human beings are carried out in view of the unified unity. This method can be called Christological anthropology. The study of humanity, to be faithful, must be done through the study of Jesus the Christ.

As chapter three pointed out, the resurrection of Jesus becomes the confirmation and vindication of the life and work of Jesus. In other words, the whole of Jesus is revealed only in the destiny of Jesus, his resurrection. It is in the light of this unified whole of Jesus' life, death and resurrection that humanity must be considered. For to consider humanity at any stage is to consider humanity only in part. Thus in any given point of human history the whole of Jesus' life and destiny is the explication of human destiny. Yet this is a provisional explication in the light of the fulfillment of human destiny in the eschaton. While Jesus' resurrection vindicated his life and work, explicating human life and destiny, it will be the eschatological resurrection of humanity that will vindicate the destiny of humanity as well as the proleptic vindication present in Jesus' own resurrection. In this way Jesus embodies the unified whole, wholly considered with humanity.

> Theology cannot be satisfied with discussing Jesus' significance for humanity in one or another individual element of Jesus' figure which, when set free from its context and isolated, perhaps acquires inappropriate significance... But theology must take into consideration the complex totality of Jesus' historical individuality and seek to formulate his universal significance.[12]

Nevertheless, while Pannenberg adheres to his concept of the whole, he also recognizes that it is at the same time one aspect or another about Jesus that will be significant for anthropological concerns in any given point of human history.[13]   It is all the more important then to insure that the individual aspects about Jesus deemed significant in a given era are always related again to the whole in and through the same Jesus Christ.

Having briefly summarized the methodological approaches of Macquarrie and of Pannenberg, five key issues appropriate to anthropology *vis à vis* Christology will now be considered. These key issues will provide the opportunity to further explicate the similarities and differences between Macquarrie and Pannenberg.

II. Key Shared Issues

Apologetics

"In a secular age one may not assume that language about God affords a universally intelligible starting point for an interpretation of the Christian faith."[14] Macquarrie reached this conclusion in a forum discussion with a physicist who had no reason or purpose for introducing "God" into any intelligible discussion.[15] Pannenberg expresses a similar absence of connectedness between the Christian faith and the secular person of the late twentieth century.

> It is difficult in secular culture to make the transition from the implicit presence of the religious theme to an explicit religious attitude because the contents of faith, particularly those of the Christian faith, have become devoid of any objective binding force in the secular consciousness.[16]

To present the Christian faith as rational and intelligible becomes one of the driving forces for both Macquarrie and Pannenberg.

Macquarrie proceeds with the apologetic task by explicating what can be known about humanity itself. Intelligible, rational anthropology lays the foundation for considering that there is something more to humanity, as chapter two pointed out. That something more is the presence of divine attributes in the attributes of humanity. Yet the transition from anthropology to theology is not a leap into speculation and irrationality.

"Some aspects of our humanity suggest a transcendent spiritual source."[17] As stated above, Macquarrie does not attempt to prove the existence of God, in the popular sense of proof, but rather to "suggest" the "possibility" of a "spiritual source." This is all very vague, but Macquarrie's purpose is to present the reasonable possibility of a reality beyond the world of humanity.

When a person considers the full range of Macquarrie's discussion of human attributes, there is sufficient basis to intelligibly consider a spiritual source and presence in these attributes. Macquarrie cites Leibniz's "principle of sufficient reason"[18] to support the adequacy of an anthropological Christology. While understanding will be implied both on the part of the thoughtful skeptic and on the part of the presenter—Macquarrie—understanding can go only so far. "There are aspects of human life and human nature which must be traced to an origin that transcends the world."[19]

Pannenberg maintains his concept of the whole in the apologetic task. All of the elements that combine together to make what is called a secular world are considered in opposition to the unified whole of the Christian faith. For Pannenberg, time is on the side of the Christian faith, because the destiny of humanity is the eschaton, revealed by the resurrection of Jesus from the dead. Because of this destiny, any other *Weltanschauung* will not stand.

Nevertheless, it is insufficient merely to oppose a secular world view with the Christian faith, and wait. That is not the same thing as confessing the faith as a Christian. In the light of the anxiety resulting from a secular meaninglessness, it is not sufficient to assume a readiness for faith as Christians understand faith. "Flight from the meaninglessness of the secular world culture into irrationality [a purely subjective Christian faith] can just as well turn to other religions and ideological elements and groups as to the church."[20]

Pannenberg sees the apologetic task then as offering a broader rational account of reality than that which secular accounts can offer. In other words, the Christian whole (unified unity) that includes the bond between humanity and God (the unifying unity) is presented intelligibly with greater rationality than the whole of a secular understanding of humanity. Thus, as chapter three demonstrated, Pannenberg does not avoid the central elements of the Christian faith. He neither accommodates nor opposes the secular culture. Rather, Pannenberg demonstrates how the life, work and resurrection of Jesus gives greater breadth and depth to human life and existence than a secular understanding can give.

Both Macquarrie and Pannenberg give nuance to St. Augustine's dictum, "We believe that we may know; we do not know that we may believe." Macquarrie and Pannenberg have altered but not abandoned this dictum. While it is true that both Macquarrie and Pannenberg assert an irrationality and subjectivity in the priority of faith for understanding, still they are not contending that faith can only follow understanding. It is not an issue of one following the other. It is an issue of one being the arena for the other. An intelligible, rational understanding about humanity and Jesus Christ is the arena in which faith may become present. Understanding about the bond between humanity and Jesus Christ is not contingent upon faith, though faith will provide rationality with a more fertile field. For both Macquarrie and Pannenberg, faith is not set in opposition to rationality, but rather faith has a greater rationality than the secular world culture hitherto has recognized.

The Incarnation

For both Macquarrie and Pannenberg there is something of a break from the traditional understanding of the incarnation. By traditional is meant an understanding of the incarnation as primarily the taking on of human flesh by the eternal Son of God in the conception and birth of Jesus.

> I come back to the point that incarnation was not a sudden, once-for-all event which happened on 25 March of the year in which the archangel Gabriel made his annunciation to the Blessed Virgin, but a process which began with creation.[21]

For Macquarrie incarnation is a process, a progressive revealing in the world, especially in humanity. What is being progressively revealed is a full humanity, revealed also in the particular human being, Jesus of Nazareth. Yet it is not only full humanity that is being revealed, but also the image of God present in humanity that is being more and more revealed as fully present. Incarnation is not simply a doctrine of the enfleshing of the eternal Λόγος, but includes both the *deification* of humanity and the *inhumanization* of divinity, as embodied in Jesus of Nazareth.

Macquarrie does not deny what Chalcedon confesses, but he wishes to say more. As already stated in chapter two, Macquarrie prefers a dynamic understanding of the term *physis*, an understanding that includes being and becoming more than it includes the static term, substance. This dynamic understanding of incarnation leads to the conclusions of the previous paragraph. Furthermore, related to this dynamic understanding, Chalcedon limits the incarnation to one point—Jesus' conception and birth. Macquarrie explicates incarnation to include not only the conception and birth of Jesus, but also the whole "Christ-event" as well as the Christian community who are participants in the "Christ-event."[22]

Jesus, then, is no new mutation suddenly appearing in the course of evolutionary time, "but the one in whom is concentrated that progressive penetration of the universe by the Logos that has been going on from the beginning."[23] This is a conclusion revealed by the consideration of humanity's attributes; revealed, in the consideration, also to have been "penetrated" by the divine Λόγος.

Pannenberg, like Macquarrie, insists on considering the incarnation in a greater light than the conception and birth of Jesus. A limiting of incarnation to the beginning of Jesus' life leads inevitably to the Christological controversies concerning the two natures in Christ—controversies, in the light of Pannenberg's apologetic task, which do not aid an intelligible defence of Christianity's breadth and depth.[24]

Instead of conception and birth, the incarnation must be considered in the light of Jesus' whole history. Furthermore, the consideration is retroactive. From the resurrection, when Jesus is confirmed as the Son of God and vindicated in all that he said and did in this office/*Amt* as the Christ, it can be seen that Jesus has been the Son from conception and birth.

Pannenberg confesses to a shift in his thought from his earlier work, *Jesus—God and Man*, to his later *Systematic Theology*.

> In 1964 I myself related the incarnation exclusively to the beginning of the earthly course of Jesus as the basis of his individual life...but we cannot do this without prejudice to the creaturely independence of Jesus in his history if this history is predetermined by an act of incarnation at the very outset.[25]

Thus, falling neither into the ancient Christological controversies about the beginning of the life of Jesus, nor into an adoptionism at the resurrection when the free creature, Jesus, becomes the Son of God, Pannenberg holds, in view of his unified unity, an incarnation as the entire history of Jesus.

Now unlike Macquarrie, the whole history of Jesus' incarnation is not a localized, actualized event of human destiny. The particularity of Jesus is a new human image antithetical to humanity.[26] The discussion of blasphemy in chapter three illustrated that Jesus is not a definite expression of universal humanity's participation with deity. Because humanity is alienated from deity by sin, it is only through Jesus—who carries the alienating charge of blasphemy for humanity—that humanity is restored to the destiny of its origins.

Again, in contrast to Macquarrie's movement from the particulars in humanity to conclusions about Jesus with humanity, Pannenberg bases his "new Adam" conclusion on the resurrection of Jesus, and through Jesus' resurrection the eschatological resurrection of restored humanity. Human destiny as the image of God is based not on the Λόγος taking flesh in the conception and birth of Jesus, but on the confirmation of Jesus' incarnation, namely, the resurrection.[27]

The Crucifixion

While there appears to be a widening gulf between Macquarrie and Pannenberg beginning from their united focus on the apologetic task discussed above, widening in their understandings of the incarnation discussed in the previous section, with the death of Jesus—and the related discussion of the resurrection in the section immediately following—a significant break occurs. Macquarrie holds a continuity between the austerity of Jesus' death on the cross and humanity's deathward being. Pannenberg explicates Jesus' death as the expiatory sacrifice for humanity's blasphemy. Macquarrie sees in Jesus' death and humanity's death the great horizon beyond which transcending humanity is carried to something more. For Pannenberg death is the absolute limit beyond which there is nothing more. For Macquarrie death is the full extent to which both humanity and deity participate with each other. For Pannenberg, any consideration of the death of God is an accommodation of Christianity to secular culture—Pannenberg holds that Jesus dies according to his human nature.[28] Nevertheless, in the midst of these antitheses, both Macquarrie and Pannenberg hold the crucifixion of Jesus as a salvific event.

As discussed in chapter two, Macquarrie defines Jesus' role as one of representative. Jesus does not suffer and die as the substitute for humanity, but rather as the representative with humanity. As representative Jesus dies as human beings die, but Jesus "holds open a place" for human death with him toward something more.

Comparison was made to Martin Luther's *theologia crucis*. Macquarrie's view reflects Luther's earlier view of the Christian's participation in the cross of Jesus. Jesus' cross is a *sacramentum et exemplum* as Luther terms it.[29] The suffering and dying Christian is united with the suffering and dying Jesus; is united with all the saints who have suffered and died. It is this participation, the death of Jesus *in nobis*, that saves. In this way the priority remains with Jesus' death as representative with humanity. "He is representative [even in transcending death] of that authentic humanity which is striving for expression in every human person."[30]

Pannenberg also considers the role of Jesus' crucifixion as representative for humanity, but Jesus is a representative very clearly *pro nobis*. The participation according to Pannenberg's *theologia crucis* is not humanity's participation in Jesus' death, but Jesus' participation on behalf of humanity in God's righteous sentence against humanity. Thus humanity is saved. In this Pannenberg echoes the later thought of Martin Luther. Luther, in 1530, wrote "So in our suffering we should so act that we give our greatest attention to the promise, in order that our cross and affliction may be turned to good."[31]

Instead of a focus on Jesus' suffering and death in the life of the Christian, Luther now focuses on God's promise through Jesus' death of salvation for the suffering and dying Christian. The mature thought of Luther's *theologia crucis* recognizes God's act of grace in and through Jesus' crucifixion on behalf of humanity. "His suffering accomplishes everything while ours does nothing."[32]

Pannenberg carries the act of God further, however. Considering Luther's mature thought as still laboring under an inaccurate penal understanding of Jesus' expiatory death, Pannenberg insists that in Jesus' death God is reconciling the world. It is a reconciliation confirmed in the resurrection of Jesus. In this Pannenberg sets aside Luther's thought.

"Only in the form of anticipation can we say that the reconciliation of the world has already taken place in the cross of Jesus."[33] Thus the cross of Jesus is salvific in the retroactive power of the resurrection. The preaching of reconciliation by the Church in view of Jesus' cross is also a proleptic reconciliation realized in the eschaton with the resurrection of the Christian.

This is Pannenberg's concept of the whole coming into play in the consideration of Jesus' crucifixion. It is an overcoming of death in the resurrection, but not the transcending through death which Macquarrie finds convincing. Rather, for Pannenberg, Jesus' death on the cross under the charge of blasphemy but vindicated by God in the resurrection, means that humanity which dies as rightly blasphemous is nonetheless given vindication through the resurrected Jesus when believing humanity too is resurrected.

The Resurrection

For Pannenberg, as chapter three demonstrated, the resurrection of Jesus is the confirmation and vindication of all that preceded the Easter event, including the incarnation of the pre-existent Son of God. This resurrection of Jesus has the retroactive power (*rückwirkende Kraft*) over all that preceded. Thus Jesus' *Amt* as the Christ has proleptic authority in his earthly ministry because of the resurrection. It is not a shadow authority but a reality in view of the resurrection confirmation.

The implication for humanity in the retroactive power of Jesus' resurrection for his pre-Easter work is great. "The resurrection of this man who had been rejected by his people and condemned [as blasphemous] and crucified by the Roman Empire freed his disciples from every unconditional tie to people and state."[34] Jesus' resurrection freed humanity, not for turning away from the present world, but for truly free service to the present world in view of the destiny of humanity, confirmed in Jesus' resurrection. For the individual human's identity confirmed in the eschatological resurrection is an already-present force through the retroactive power of Jesus' resurrection considered with the whole of human eschatology. "Now for me to live is Christ, and to die is gain." (Philippians 1:21)

Pannenberg's insistence on an historical verifiability of Jesus' resurrection is more than a defense of his own methodology. "For if Christ has not been raised...we are to be pitied." (See I Corinthians 15:12-19) The unified unity of Jesus and humanity demands a verified historical resurrection of Jesus as the confirmation of his life and work, providing the basis—provisional until the eschaton—for the retroactive power of the eschaton present in the historical life of the Christian. Again, with an apologetic purpose in Pannenberg's mind, there can be no retreating into an irrational faith.[35] Anthropology considered historically must always be considered Christologically.

For Macquarrie, as chapter two stated, the resurrection is a very difficult idea to accept.[36]   Resurrection is something that surpasses human experience and is a subject that forces one to enter speculation. As Macquarrie's method has built on the progression from what is known to what is possible, resurrection, becomes just such a possibility. "Perhaps [it] is transcendence to a new level of being of the human person, a level which eludes our understanding so long as we are seeing it only from below."[37]

For this reason Macquarrie prefers his "Austere Ending" to the life of Jesus.   He does not wish to deny a place to the "Happy Ending" which includes the resurrection, but human experience forces him to consider other possibilities.   The entire discussion of transcendence is just such a possibility.   The unified attributes of human beings combine in the face of limits to propel the human being in freedom to move beyond to something more.   Death, as Macquarrie often states, is a limit that also must be overcome toward the potential of something more. But unable to explicate the precise nature of what something more beyond death might be, resurrection is an acceptable term for considering the something more in humanity's "from below" vantage point.

Because of the desire not to enter highly speculative discussions, Macquarrie limits resurrection implications to what can be known. The new life of the crucified Jesus living in the Christian community is one "something more" that has transcended Jesus' own death.   "This new community which began with the incarnation and with Christ's victory over the powers of sin and evil is the ever-expanding center in which Christ's revealing work continues."[38]   Macquarrie might be pressed to say that the Christian community is the life Jesus now lives, having transcended death.

Thus, in the living community, the body of Christ, the apostolic references to baptism as a being in Christ and to the Lord's Supper as uniting the recipient with the life of Christ are reflections of how the resurrection is explicated in something more, but a something more which is accessible to humanity "from below" rather than in speculation about a humanly incomprehensible resurrection life.

The Future

From what has been said by way of summary, comparing Macquarrie and Pannenberg to this point, their understanding of the future has been present in their explication of anthropology and Christology, especially regarding their understanding of the resurrection. The language used by Macquarrie and Pannenberg, illustrate their differing views of the future. Macquarrie uses terms which view the future as evolving from the present—terms such as possibility, potential, freedom and transcendence. Pannenberg speaks of a determined future toward which the present evolves—terms such as destiny, retroactive power, prolepsis, confirmation and vindication. Macquarrie views the future as open possibility from the present. Pannenberg considers the future as a yet-to-be-fully-known destiny progressively revealed in the present.

Nevertheless, both Macquarrie and Pannenberg hold one issue in common. Both do not regard the present as isolated. For Pannenberg, the present for humanity is provisional until confirmation by the eschaton. For Macquarrie, humanity's present is not static, but rather is a becoming either more or less human.

Pannenberg's present is provisional not because the future destiny of humanity is in question, but because that destiny has not been actualized. In view of the part—humanity—the future is provisional. In view of the unified unity the destiny is not provisional but rather proleptically present. The present is, then, an appearance of what will be. But considered in view of the whole, this appearance is that same reality already present. Pannenberg calls this "anticipation"—the future is already present in its anticipation. But anticipation is always ambiguous.[39]

Macquarrie, on the other hand, does not speak of the future in any linear manner as Pannenberg does. With his language of possibility and potential, Macquarrie views what may be called future in the light of human creativity. Humanity goes beyond each hitherto known present to a something more. As such "the human being is the bearer of the world's potential."[40] The future is not so much a time as an unfixed process of self-creation by humanity. This concept flows out of Macquarrie's anthropological foundation outlined in chapter two.

Nevertheless, since death is transcended to something more, as Macquarrie's discussion of Christology and resurrection has shown, the future is not something merely for those human beings who will live in years yet to come. Macquarrie's "body of Christ" language in the Christian community implies the something more of human life transcending death. This organic something more is not pantheism—all is God, God is all. Rather, Macquarrie prefers the term "panentheism." This concept carries the future with it. In panentheism God is neither a natural power in all things nor a spiritual being apart from nature. "He is conceived as manifesting himself alike in the whole process of nature and in the process of spirit as it rises above nature."[41] This manifesting process in panentheism captures Macquarrie's concept of future—both for humanity and for God.

III. Synthesis or Paradox?

In the introductory chapter the intention of this book was stated. The explication of the twin subjects of anthropology and Christology in the thought of John Macquarrie and Wolfhart Pannenberg would serve as a comparison of the two theologians' views. Numerous issues of common interest between Macquarrie and Pannenberg have enabled such an approach to be made. In comparison, however, significant differences have been disclosed.

For Macquarrie, Christological implications derived by a thorough study of anthropology has resulted in a strong emphasis on a Christology *in nobis*. The attributes of human beings that distinguish human life from animal life provide the basis for understanding the nature and work of Jesus Christ. The difference between Jesus and universal humanity is a difference of degree not kind. What is *in Jesus* is also *in nobis*, in humanity; realized fully in Jesus, however.

The work of Jesus Christ, fully human, is a work done as representative of humanity. Neither outside human experience as substitute nor outside humanity as example, the life and work of Jesus Christ is *exemplum et sacramentum*, that is, involved in humanity most intimately. In the person of Jesus a transcending humanity from below is met by a transcending deity from above. This sacramental meeting in Jesus is not, however, something outside humanity, *pro nobis*. It is, rather, the revelation of what is happening in humanity, *in nobis*. Revealed in the attributes of humanity, both humanity and deity share being. This means that the infinite is reflected in the finite (*finitum capax infiniti*). This also means that there is not an absolute discontinuity between God and humanity. With such a "shared being" understanding, God becomes a God working and suffering in and with his creation rather than standing over it. For Macquarrie this concept of God is very close to the God of Christian faith.[42]

Does not such a strong emphasis on human beings and the work of Jesus Christ *in nobis* render Jesus ultimately superfluous? If Jesus Christ is the revelation of what is already in humanity, will not time alone bring about the same result of a transcending humanity meeting a transcending deity without Jesus Christ?

Macquarrie frequently emphasizes the difference between humanity and Jesus as a difference of degree, not kind. At the same time he denies an infinite qualitative difference between deity and humanity because God has entered the human life named Jesus. Thus, on the part of humanity, Jesus brings to light what has been possible in humanity though not realized until the life of Jesus, namely the participation of humanity with deity. Furthermore, on the part of deity, Jesus brings to light what has been possible in deity but not realized until the life of Jesus, namely, participation of deity with humanity. Thus, while this potential is present *in nobis* and *in dei*, it is realized *in Jesus*—a Jesus differing only in degree from humanity and deity. The potential for participation by transcending humanity and transcending deity is present *in nobis*, realized through Jesus *in nobis*, but realized only because of Jesus Christ. In this way, Macquarrie's anthropological Christology confesses a Savior very truly *in nobis*, in humanity.

For Pannenberg, the emphasis has been on a Jesus Christ *pro nobis*, for humanity. Pannenberg begins his method with Christology and moves to anthropology. His explication of the life, work and destiny of Jesus Christ results in a representative Savior, but representative for humanity, *pro nobis*. It is the resurrection of Jesus, his destiny, that vindicates the work of Jesus as the Christ. His destiny-vindicated work reveals humanity's destiny; humanity's destiny will likewise vindicate Jesus' work *pro nobis*.

While Pannenberg's concept of the whole, the unified unity, rightly sets Christology and anthropology very intimately, there does remain a break between the destiny of humanity with Jesus and human destiny without Jesus. The discussion in Pannenberg about blasphemy and the vicarious atonement of Jesus Christ for humanity's guilt of blasphemy emphasizes the break. Thus while throughout Pannenberg's writing there is a proleptic element for both Jesus and humanity *vis á vis* the eschaton—a proleptic element that is intimately tied to both Jesus and humanity—nevertheless, the *Amt* of Jesus as the Christ is very definitely a work *pro nobis*.

The benefits of Jesus' *Amt, pro nobis*, are seen in humanity's destiny.   In Pannenberg's Christological anthropology humanity's anxiety is overcome by Jesus' destiny *pro nobis*. Humanity's guilt of blasphemy is overcome by Jesus' vicarious sacrifice, *pro nobis*. Humanity's end in death is overcome by Jesus' confirming resurrection, *pro nobis*. There is in Pannenberg a desire to emphasize very strongly the human element in Jesus, but in every detail the human with humanity is considered and confessed in a Jesus Christ for humanity, *pro nobis*.

Thus the comparison between Macquarrie and Pannenberg is paradoxical—*in nobis* and *pro nobis*.[43] As with paradoxes, the desire to combine the two is strong but must be resisted.   To add to Macquarrie's thought the *pro nobis* of Pannenberg's method would compromise, for Macquarrie, humanity's image of God as bearers of deity; would compromise the potential of humanity to be fully human in itself as the creation of God. To add to Pannenberg's thought the *in nobis* of Macquarrie's method would compromise, for Pannenberg, the act of God as the unifying unity vindicating the destiny of Jesus in his resurrection and, through Jesus, the vindication of humanity's new destiny in the eschaton.

Having said this, however, a synthesis in their methods is possible. Macquarrie's method is to consider the present as directed toward an open future of possibility. Pannenberg's method is a destined future being revealed proleptically in the considered present. Because of the provisional quality of both Macquarrie's and Pannenberg's methods—Macquarrie because of his emphasis on possibility; Pannenberg because of his emphasis on eschatological confirmation— one might conclude, synthetically, that what Macquarrie posits as possibility, Pannenberg explicates as proleptic destiny. What will be has been all along; what is is what will be. This is not a meaningless conclusion, but rather a provisional thought in the light of the paradoxical nature of Macquarrie's and Pannenberg's methods.

Nevertheless, because a synthesis risks compromising the paradox presented in both Macquarrie and Pannenberg, Luther's concept of *simul* was suggested in the introductory chapter instead of a pure synthesis.

The familiar use of the term in Luther concerns the Christian as *simul justus et peccator*, the Christian is simultaneously righteous and a sinner. It is a simultaneity that is not part and part—part righteous, part sinner—but *totus justus* and *totus peccator*. Furthermore, when considered from below, the Christian is also *semper justus* and *semper peccator*. In this way the integrity of the confession of righteousness and sinfulness is maintained by means of the word *simul*.

Macquarrie's anthropological Christology and Pannenberg's Christological anthropology demonstrate such a *simul—simul in nobis et pro nobis*. The potential of transcendence, brought to light fully in Jesus, is totally found in humanity; not partly so, but fully so in possibility. Yet the destiny of humanity revealed proleptically in the confirming destiny of Jesus is fully on behalf of humanity; not partly so, but fully so as the act of God. Furthermore, when considered from below with humanity as the arena for both Macquarrie and Pannenberg in their methods, the image of God dictates for Macquarrie a *semper in nobis*, while for Pannenberg the image of God is *semper pro nobis*. Thus, in the final analysis both Macquarrie's anthropological Christology and Pannenberg's Christological anthropology must be considered fully, yet simultaneously. *Simul et semper in nobis et pro nobis.*

Notes

1. Macquarrie, *Jesus Christ in Modern Thought*, x.

2. Macquarrie, *In Search of Humanity*, 6.

3. Ibid., 9.

4. Ibid.

5. Ibid., 2.

6. Ibid., 256.

7. Macquarrie, *Jesus Christ in Modern Thought*, 372.

8. Ibid., 372.

9. Pannenberg, *Metaphysics and the Idea of God*, 142.

10. Ibid., 143.

11. Ibid., 146.

12. Pannenberg, *Jesus—God and Man*, 204.

13. Ibid.

14. Macquarrie, *Studies in Christian Existentialism*, 4.

15. Ibid., 3.

16. Wolfhart Pannenberg, *Christianity in a Secularized World* (New York: The Crossroad Publishing Co., 1989), 44.

17. Macquarrie, *In Search of Humanity*, 258.

18. Ibid., 258.

19. Ibid., 258-259.

20. Pannenberg, *Christianity in a Secularized World*, 57.

21. Macquarrie, *Jesus Christ in Modern Thought*, 392.

22. Ibid., 393.

23. Ibid., 394.

24. Pannenberg, *Christianity in a Secularized World*, 58.

25. Pannenberg, *Systematic Theology, Vol. 2*, 384-385n173.

26. Ibid., 295.

27. Ibid., 225.

28. Pannenberg, *Christianity in a Secularized World*, 50.

29. Martin Luther, "The Blessed Sacrament of the Holy and True Body of Christ, and the Brotherhoods, 1519," *Luther's Works, Vol. 31* (Philadelphia: Fortress Press, 1960), 564.

30. Macquarrie, *Jesus Christ in Modern Thought*, 401.

31. Martin Luther, "Sermon on Cross and Suffering, 1530," *Luther's Works, Vol. 51* (Philadelphia: Fortress Press, 1959), 201.

32. Ibid., 208.

33. Pannenberg, *Systematic Theology, Vol. 2*, 412-413.

34. Pannenberg, *Anthropology in Theological Perspective*, 480.

35. "Christianity may not be content with just securing the existence of the dogmatic content of the tradition... It is a temptation for church and theology to regard as an opportunity for faith the readiness of human beings to succumb to the irrational, to an irrationally affirmed counterworld, as a result of a feeling of alienation in the secular world of culture... Rather, the opportunity for Christianity and its theology is...to offer the reduced rationality of secular culture a greater breadth of reason, which would also include the horizon of the bond between humankind and God." Pannenberg, *Christianity in a Secularized World*, 57.

36. Macquarrie, *Jesus Christ in Modern Thought*, 406.

37. Ibid., 409.

38. Macquarrie, *Principles of Christian Theology*, 326.

39. Pannenberg, *Metaphysics and the Idea of God*, 96.

40. Macquarrie, *Jesus Christ in Modern Thought*, 367.

41. Ibid., 233.

42. Macquarrie, *In Search of Humanity*, 257.

43. It is very much like the God-man paradox, which Kierkegaard called "the absolute paradox." *In nobis* and *pro nobis* present a tension and opposition. Macquarrie's words also are applicable here: "The paradox [of the God-man]

cannot be dissolved; it is inherent in the attempt by finite minds to reflect on ultimate issues. But even so we have a duty to reflect as deeply as possible and to show, so far as we can, that the paradox is a dialectical conjunction of opposites and not sheer nonsense or irreconcilable contradiction." Macquarrie, *Principles of Christian Theology*, 306.

Bibliography

Primary Sources

Macquarrie, John. *Studies in Christian Existentialism.*
London: SCM Press, Ltd., 1965.

_____. "Christianity Without Incarnation? Some Critical
Comments." *The Truth of God Incarnate.* Edited by Michael
Green. London: Hodder and Stoughton, 1977.

_____. *Principles of Christian Theology.* 2nd ed.
New York: Charles Scribner's Sons, 1977.

_____. *Christian Hope.*
New York: Seabury Press, 1978.

_____. *The Humility of God.*
London: SCM Press, Ltd., 1978.

_____. "The Humility of God." *The Myth/Truth of God
Incarnate.* Edited by Durstan R. McDonald. Wilton, Connecticut:
Morehouse-Barlow, Co. Inc., 1979.

_____. *In Search of Humanity.*
New York: The Crossroad Publishing Co., 1983.

_____. *In Search of Deity.*
New York: The Crossroad Publishing Co., 1984.

_____. *Jesus Christ in Modern Thought.*
London: SCM Press, Ltd., 1990.

Pannenberg, Wolfhart. *Grundzüge der Christologie.*
Gütersloh: Gütersloh Verlagshaus Gerd Mohn, 1964.

_____. *Jesus—God and Man.*
Philadelphia: Westminster Press, 1968.

_____. *Anthropology in Theological Perspective.*
Philadelphia: Westminster Press, 1985.

Pannenberg, Wolfhart. *Metaphysics and the Idea of God.*
Grand Rapids, Michigan: Wm. B. Eerdmans Publishing Co., 1988.

_____. *Systematische Theologie, Bände 1-3.*
Göttingen: Vandenhoeck & Ruprecht, 1988.

_____. *Christianity in a Secularized World.*
New York: The Crossroad Publishing Co., 1989.

_____. *An Introduction to Systematic Theology.*
Grand Rapids, Michigan: Wm. B. Eerdmans Publishing Co., 1991.

_____. *Systematic Theology, Volume 1.*
Grand Rapids, Michigan: Wm. B. Eerdmans Publishing Co., 1991.

_____. *Systematic Theology, Volume 2.*
Grand Rapids, Michigan: Wm. B. Eerdmans Publishing Co., 1994.

_____. *Systematic Theology, Volume 3.*
Grand Rapids, Michigan: Wm. B. Eerdmans Publishing Co., 1997.

Secondary Literature

Braaten, Carl E. "The Current Controversy on Revelation:
Pannenberg and His Critics," *Journal of Religion* 45 (1965): 225-237.

Brown, Colin. *Miracles and the Critical Mind.*
Grand Rapids, Michigan: Wm. B. Eerdmans Publishing Co., 1984.

Clayton, Philip & Braaten, Carl E., editors. *The Theology of Wolfhart Pannenberg.* Minneapolis: Augsburg Publishing House, 1988.

Cobb, John B. Jr. "Pannenberg's Resurrection Christology: A Critique," *Theological Studies* 35 (1974): 711-721.

_____. "Wolfhart Pannenberg's *Jesus—God and Man,*" *Journal of Religion* 49 (1969): 192-201.

Galloway, Allan D. *Wolfhart Pannenberg.*
London: George Allen & Unwin, Ltd., 1973.

Grenz, Stanley. *Reason For Hope: The Systematic Theology of Wolfhart Pannenberg.* New York: Oxford University Press, 1990.

Hefling, Charles C. "Reviving Adamic Adoptionism: The Example of John Macquarrie." *Theological Studies* 52 (S 1991): 476-94.

Jenkins, David. *The Scope and Limits of John Macquarrie's Existential Philosophy.* Washington D.C.: University Press of America, 1987.

Kee, Alister & Long, Eugene T., editors. *Being and Truth: Essays in Honor of John Macquarrie.* London: SCM Press Ltd., 1986.

Long, Eugene T. *Existence, Being and God.*
New York: Paragon House Publishers, 1985.

Luther, Martin. "Career of the Reformer I." *Luther's Works, Volume 31.* Philadelphia: Fortress Press, 1957.

_____. "Word and Sacrament I." *Luther's Works, Volume 35.* Philadelphia: Fortress Press, 1960.

_____. "Sermons I." *Luther's Works, Volume 51.* Philadelphia: Fortress Press, 1959.

Macquarrie, John. "Theologies of Hope: A Critical Examination," *Expository Times* 82 (1971): 100-105.

Macquarrie, John. "What Is a Human Being?" Review of W. Pannenberg, *Anthropology in Theological Perspective, Expository Times* 97 (1986): 202-203.

McKenzie, David. *Wolfhart Pannenberg and Religious Philosophy.* Washington D.C.: University Press of America, 1980.

Olive, Don H. *Wolfhart Pannenberg.*
    Waco, Texas: Word, 1973.

Olson, Roger E. "Pannenberg's Theological Anthropology: A Review
    Article," *Perspectives in Religious Studies* 13 (1986): 161-169.

Walsh, Brian J. "A Critical Review of Pannenberg's *Anthropology in
    Theological Perspective,*" *Christian Scholar's Review* 15 (1986):
    247-259.

Index